Mon cher amour chéri,

Je t'ai dit hier soir que nous avions trouvé le [...]
u aider à réaliser nos désirs suprêmes et je me demande [...]
te satisfaire !.. J'ai eu la vague, mais douloureuse m[...]
chose se rébellant en toi à l'idée que j'avais [...]
avais pu demander

[...]ude,   chère, [...]
[...]riste à la pensée
[...]is combien je t'a[...]   amour chéri,
[...]e fois plus heu[...]
[...]donnée depu[...]   Les jours se suivent mais hélas !
[...], moi unique[...]   Hier, à la même heure, nous étions ré[...]
[...] chéri plus a[...]   nid si calme et nous nous aimions [...]
[...] de moy au[...]   toutes les folies que nous avons faites ont [...]
[...]les co[...]   la voluptueuse combature des lendemains [...]
                           fatigue m'est bien chère car elle prolonge [...]
           de ces ardents baisers.

                           Aujourd'hui je n'ai pu que te regarde[...]
ce matin ! seconde fugitive a suffi pour emplir ma[...]
[...]ncher dans[...] et je continue à penser à toi, à nous.. avec la [...]
[...] te vois, même tendresse !....
[...]rosions sor   Sais-tu, mon cher chéri, tout ce que t[...]
[...]dra sur [...]   Sais-tu que [...] que jamais tu as comblé [...]
[...]ond de tr[...]   bas, aneanti [...]
chère ta[...]   [...]ment tant les [...]
vie ... q[...]omment veux tu, mon cher aimé quel[...]

THE PASSION OF MADEMOISELLE S.

THE PASSION OF MADEMOISELLE S.

LETTERS TO A LOVER

Edited and introduced by
Jean-Yves Berthault

Translated by Adriana Hunter

WILLIAM HEINEMANN: LONDON

1 3 5 7 9 10 8 6 4 2

William Heinemann
20 Vauxhall Bridge Road
London SW1V 2SA

William Heinemann is part of the Penguin Random House
group of companies whose addresses can be found at
global.penguinrandomhouse.com.

Translation © Adriana Hunter

Introduction and Notes © Jean-Yves Berthault 2016

First published by William Heinemann in 2016.
First published in France by Éditions Gallimard-Versilio in 2015.

www.randomhouse.co.uk

A CIP catalogue record for this book is available from the British Library.

ISBN 9781785150180 (Hardback)
ISBN 9781785150197 (Trade Paperback)

Typeset by Palimpsest Book Production Ltd, Falkirk, Stirlingshire

Printed and bound by Clays Ltd, St Ives plc

Penguin Random House is committed to a sustainable future for
our business, our readers and our planet. This book is made from
Forest Stewardship Council® certified paper.

THE PASSION OF MADEMOISELLE S.

PREFACE

While helping a friend clear out an apartment with a forgotten cellar, I noticed a packing case behind a pile of wood. I moved aside a few broken old picture frames and the odd chair with a missing foot, and found the case was filled with empty preserving jars between two thick layers of newspaper. I felt no one would go to so much trouble to protect a few unused jars with no lids. What if they'd been put there to hide some fantastical treasure?

I had the unusual feeling that an extraordinary adventure lay right there at my fingertips, that something significant was happening, like when you can feel the hand of fate or you believe you've witnessed a miracle; it was one of those goosebump moments. It could have been a treasure map or an old woollen stocking filled with hundreds of silver coins, share certificates for companies long since collapsed, the private diary of a now dead young lady or an unknown Mozart score. So I ploughed hastily through the layers of paper and jars guarding the bottom of the box, and came to a heavy leather bag, a beautiful thing with initials engraved on it in silver. And inside, so many letters, all in the same handwriting, in no particular order.

I started to read one, then another, and would eventually explore the entire correspondence of what were clearly love letters, written not merely in daring terms but with extraordinary erotic audacity. They had been deliberately kept together in this satchel which, by all appearances, was intended to remain hidden. On one of the letters I spotted a date: 1929. And they were all signed by a woman – Simone.

Consumed with curiosity, I bought the letters from my friend. This book is a selection of these letters that Simone wrote to her married lover Charles. Only a few of them are dated, and it took me almost a year to establish their chronology, making the most of an ambassadorship in a relatively quiet country which allowed me to devote my weekends and many an evening to the exercise. Given that the correspondence is very extensive, I have selected only a limited number of letters (a little over a third) to include in this volume and, for reasons of discretion, names and places mentioned have been changed.

There are many possible readings of this epistolary collection . . .

On the surface, it could be read as one woman's salacious

relationship with her lover, expressed in the coarsest of terms, something to be read with the avid curiosity that an anachronistic pornographic novel might arouse. Simone's vocabulary grows more deliberately risqué with the passing months, which is surprising from a cultured young lady, particularly one who, judging by all the evidence, was from a 'good family'. What explanation can there be for such excesses and such 'modern'-sounding language? And what sort of woman would have written like that in those days?

I showed these letters to a friend before their publication, and he said: 'Come on, admit it, you wrote these! They cannot have been written by a woman in 1928!' and I had to show him the original correspondence on its faded writing paper for him to believe me.

Where then did Simone learn the obscene vocabulary that she so openly drops into her elegant turns of phrase? I would conjecture that allowing this vocabulary to intrude into her naturally chaste words constituted a necessary transgression if she were to overcome the obstacles to her own sexual fulfilment. She most likely adopted words that Charles let slip in the heat of passion, because at the time a man would have allowed himself to say things to his mistress that he would not have said to his wife; and in her quest for liberation, Simone must have appropriated this 'male' vocabulary. We can only imagine that this emancipation, which was so incongruous for the period, must have had an aphrodisiac effect on Charles. The freedom with which they spoke opened up many new possibilities for both lovers. They had overcome a powerful taboo: vocalising their experiences.

It would seem that this verbal audacity was introduced at the same time as the acts themselves, with one form of transgression preceding and fuelling the other, and so we would not find its source in the books that might have been found on Simone's shelf at the time, which I would guess contained mostly classics. Instead we should trace it to her psyche or the collective subconscious of the time. Indeed, however extensively we explore the most daring literature of the period, it seems nothing on Simone's shelves could have inspired her use of such terms. At the time these letters were written (1928–30), Jean Genet (1910–86) was embarking on his career as a petty criminal rather than a writer, and had not yet had anything published. Pierre Louÿs (1870–1925) did not go to such extremes; André Gide (1869–1951) published *Corydon* in 1924 and *Si le grain ne meurt* (*If I Die*) in 1926, but he touched only lightly on his homosexual obsessions, and *The Songs of Bilitis* was not yet bedside reading for the upper-middle classes. In any event, none of these books resorted to language that would certainly have been deemed obscene in its day.

But Simone was revelling in this emerging world; she was a contemporary of the first silent pornographic films and of *La Revue nègre*, a musical show created in 1925 by a black woman, Josephine Baker, who scandalised the world by dancing with a banana belt as her only clothing, quickly becoming world-famous. During this period, thousands of pornographic photographs and some short films were passed around in Paris, sold under the counter at affordable prices.

This was all part of the hedonistic fame of Paris in the 1920s, a scene that was brimming with all sorts of artistic experiments that revolutionised social mores, and of a society that – perhaps in spite of itself – was witnessing the advent of an immoral 'new order' in Paris. In 1917, Marcel Duchamp had pushed the boundaries of art by exhibiting a urinal, entitled *Fountain*; in 1920, the first Dada manifestations took place in Paris, followed in 1925 by the first surrealist exhibition. Meanwhile the Ballets Russes were enthralling the Parisian elite. At the time of Simone and Charles's correspondence, Paris was the global art capital, and there were no limits on creativity. Our two young lovers are therefore an expression of this, some twenty years after the separation between the church and the state.

One of the merits of this remarkable document is that it takes us deep into the lives of women who have at last been emancipated, and into the mind of one 'flapper' as she comes to terms with who she is, and shamelessly reveals the appeal of the new freedoms offered by the Roaring Twenties. These letters are a remarkable illustration of why Parisiennes fully deserved the reputation they had earned since the turn of the twentieth century and on into the interwar years. The letters endorse the fact that physical urges are only fleeting and emotions more enduring, and they emphatically demonstrate something that we already suspect: that our contemporary world, which prides itself on having invented everything, is simply stumbling through the same endlessly repeated round of redundant human instincts and aspirations.

But what I personally find truly captivating about this correspondence, what stays with me and what I hope to offer the reader, is that it is above all else a magnificent but tragic love story shot through with an obsessive neurosis. I find it profoundly moving, and believe that, for the sake of Simone's feelings and her sacrifices (rather than for her wild excesses), this woman who suffered such pain deserves to be brought back to life, and that this aspect of her obscure and painful life should be recognised after her death.

I have to confess I take great pleasure in publishing this volume just as my career as an ambassador comes to an end. Like Simone, I'm a nonconformist.

JYB
January 2016

1928

Saturday, 11.30 a.m.

Forgive me, darling, if this note is too brief . . . I am
short of time, because you know I would have plenty
to say to you if only I could!

Today you will have only tender thoughts from
me, only a kiss on your beloved lips and your pretty
brown eyes, but I shall be by your side in spirit. And
you, beloved, will you think of me? Yes, I hope so, and
I do hope to have a little note from you in Monday's
post.

Darling, I should like to see you one evening this week
if at all possible because I so long for your touch that it
will be too endless to wait until Saturday.

I want another taste of the passionate moments of our
last meeting . . . the memory of your touch is peculiarly
unsettling to me, and I want to be in your arms again
feeling the wonderful sensations you give me. Loved
one, I want you to love me with all the ardour of your
desire, I want you to make me come furiously with
your perverse couplings. Beloved darling, tell me that,
like me, you want to feel my touch again, tell me also
that you are happy in my arms, so very happy, and that
you love me . . .

Be good, my adored lover. Keep your perverted fondling for me, keep it for me alone, I want to love you like that forever and ever.

Goodbye, my beloved little god. Till Monday I hope!

Give me your wonderful body, I want to hold it in my arms, hold it tight until I am imbued with its intoxicating smell. I am pressing my lips to yours in a deep kiss that comes from the bottom of my heart, my heart which is filled with you, nothing but you.

All my most tender thoughts, my loved one. I love you.

Simone

My darling love,

How wonderful yesterday evening was . . . All that time spent close to you had aroused me, and your *pneumatique*[1] was enough to intoxicate me altogether.

---

1   *Pneumatiques*, better known by the diminutive term *pneus*, were a very Parisian means of transmitting mail. They were devised in 1866 by Henri Rouart, a painter, inventor and industrialist, in order to provide a link between the Grand Hotel near the opera house and the Bourse (the Paris stock exchange). Aside from this initial usage, they began to be used more widely in 1879 and were not phased out until 1984, supplanted by faxes and then emails. One hundred and twenty post offices had the infrastructure to send letters via a system of compressed air tubes, travelling up to 1 km per minute. The user would buy a pre-stamped sheet from a post office and could write up to twenty lines on one side of the sheet; this was then folded by sticking together the edges, and the address was written on the other side. The tubes of compressed air formed a network all over Paris, and only minutes after the letter had been sent a postman would be on hand to deliver the *pneu* to the addressee. In its day it was a means of communicating in 'real time'. Although they have disappeared from modern-day post offices, such systems are still in use in some French institutions and large government offices. When I was a junior diplomat at the Ministry of Foreign Affairs, once or twice a year it was part of your service to do a night shift in a very spartan room next to the minister's palace. You would be

All those passionate words were deliciously exciting, and once I was in my great big bed in the dark of my own room, I was not very well behaved. I perfumed my whole body before slipping between those cool sheets, as if you were to come and join me there.

With my head on my pillow I conjure images of my darling little god. I run one hand slowly over my entire body which gradually starts to quiver. My hand moves from my breasts down to my thighs, drifting briefly into the warm pelt and then sliding further down. Under the effects of a double fondling, a boundless sense of delight steals over every inch of me. I am shivering with pleasure at this stage because I am thinking of you with all my might. When I come it is so powerful I have to restrain myself from crying out. Charles, darling Charles, yes, tomorrow I shall treat you to the enticing performance you so long to see. When I reach my devastating climax, you will take all of me so I have no time to recover, so that a second climax still stronger than the first carries me deeper into pleasure.

Tomorrow, darling beloved, we can act out all our fantasies.

---

awakened throughout the night by the horrendous noise of the plastic tubes containing emergency cables that would fall into their compartments just above the small bed. An inconvenience that has now been forgotten, thanks to the emergence of more silent, electronic devices.

I have to stop again. I do not have time to say everything I should like to say.

Till later, my loved one. I love you.

Simone

Tuesday, 31 July

My dear darling,

Thank you for your last long letter. You are a darling writing to me like that, it makes me so happy when I see the little white envelope in the box! I too would have been very sad had you not replied straight away . . . I love you! My dear love, I simply cannot get away from here before Sunday evening. Believe me, my beloved, just like you I ardently long for our next tryst. Every ounce of my being is straining towards you, calling to the exquisite lover that you are, that you will always be. No, darling love, I shall never tire of you, you can be sure of that. I have been too happy in your arms and I already know what pleasure I shall feel when you take me again . . . I am already envisioning our next meeting. You will make me suffer cruelly, my body belongs to you and it will squirm beneath your blows, you will hear me begging for mercy . . . And your longing for me will be all the more violent because I shall press my skin against yours, I shall wrap all of you in my quivering thighs, my mouth will seek out your lips to bruise them with fierce kisses. My loved one, you will take me the way you like best, and our

14

passionate embrace will transport us both to the bound-less pleasure that only such embraces can bring. The most perverse of couplings, you say? What of it, darling Charles, what I want above all else is for you to be happy in my arms. So I am at your orders, my darling master! If you only knew how I long to nestle in your arms! I so want to be back beside your body which has afforded me such ecstasies . . .

Darling loved one, just you wait and see how we love each other after this long separation, so close to each other but unable to be united . . . Oh! Why can you not be free this evening? What wonderful times we would spend together in each other's arms, in the quiet half-light of this big bedroom, pressed up against each other after the wild ecstasy that leaves us both powerless; when our violent mutual desire has transported us to supreme pinnacles of pleasure, how marvellous we shall feel, my love, resting in this big bed . . . We must wait till Saturday next to savour such wild embraces. I am fretting over something, darling. You see, I do wonder where we can meet once my family has returned . . . For I do not believe we could part so hastily, my love; you may not be able to tear yourself away from me, but neither can I turn away from your touch . . . we shall have to think about this problem. We can talk about it in Paris – would you mind? My love, I must go. Write me a long letter I can read before I leave here. I have not had any photographs taken of myself, my darling.

Goodbye, darling treasure, I send you my most fervent kisses all over, everywhere. And I shall say till Monday, my loved one.

I love you helplessly, my adorable lover.

Your Simone

My darling friend,
    This is also the last letter you will have from me.
In two days I take the train for Paris,[2] towards you, my
love, whom I cannot wait to hold to my heart after such
a long absence. You cannot imagine how I have missed
you over these twenty-three days spent far from you.
Many a day I was sad despite the beautiful landscape – all
its charms combined left me unmoved! Were it not for
your dear letters telling me you love me, allowing me to
relive all our most wonderful moments, I should have
been sadder still!

    Do you want me to talk to you of our love? There are
no words, however eloquent, to express all the passion, all
the fire, all the madness contained within those two words:
'our love'. We share such beautiful times together, we taste

---

2 As this is summer, it is likely that Simone is returning to Paris
   from a holiday, probably spent in the company of her family,
   either on the French Riviera or near Biarritz. Both were
   becoming increasingly popular holiday destinations, and at
   this time were mostly frequented by British people, who had
   recently discovered the delights of the French coast, and by
   the well-to-do French population.

such ecstasies that it would be ill-advised even to attempt to describe them! What more can I tell you, my dear love, other than I feel I must be dreaming when I think of everything that makes up 'our love'. You have allowed me to experience unforgettable sensations, you and all your perversity have managed to wake in me goodness knows what secret instincts which now make me long for new, still more perverted and powerful pleasures. You are a master in the very delicate art of lovemaking and I too am so happy, so happy that I have managed to secure you.

I imagined nothing during this absence, nothing, I simply remembered. And I know that when our bodies are together again, when your skin comes close to mine, such a shudder of desire will steal through me that it will dictate every possible excess to me! Yes, I love you with an absolute love, I love you with my heart but also and especially with my senses, with my flesh, and I want all of you, do you hear, dear love. I do not want any secret recesses of your body to escape my touch and my kisses! It is a madness that suddenly grips me when I have you, here, quite naked and so beautiful in my arms. Oh, beloved darling, let me do it, let me stroke you all over, everywhere. I want to kiss all of you so wildly, your smooth white skin, these firm thighs, this stomach and this adorable chest where my blazing cheek seeks out cooler skin. If you want to experience devastating sensations, talk, dictate, and I shall obey. Happy, so happy to hear you groaning with desire and pleasure.

While my heart flutters with delicious agitation, I am here waiting for your first embrace. You will make me suffer, you say. So be it, but tell me you will be happy in my arms, that I shall hear your cry of victory, your male cry, when you have me in your arms, battered, beaten, exhausted!

I belong to you, my beloved lover, with all the might of flesh intoxicated by your brutal ministrations . . . As you know, I accept your fierce passions in advance if they can unite us all the more completely. I too have tasted the most voluptuously intense sensations in your arms. I have climaxed with all my might under your blows and brutalities. Mostly I have climaxed from your skilled possession of me. I want to experience such climaxes again, the like of which I have never known in the ordinary coupling which leaves me cold and numb. I *never* want to experience it with you, do you hear? Because *I know* we would both be disappointed. And it would lower us to the level of ordinary lovers while we currently glide through forbidden planes, we are lawless, depraved, passionate; all things that make up 'our love'.

Alas, dear darling love, I cannot free myself of my duties to savour exquisite moments in your arms! It is as impossible for me as it is for you. I have to go to the office[3] at eight in the morning, as soon as my train arrives.

---

3 A great many women, who had replaced men on farms or factories during the First World War, had been sent back to

We shall have to wait till Saturday, and be very patient, my loved one! But if you were kind you could pass by the office for five minutes to see me, or you could telephone[4] so that at least I could hear your voice!

---

their households after the end of the war. The government was eager to help increase the birth rate at any cost after the catastrophic losses on the battlefield of 1,400,000 men, 27 per cent of those aged 18–27. Female workers represented only 30 per cent of the total workforce at the end of the decade. However, there was nothing unusual about an upper-class woman working in an office in 1920s Paris. Women of the upper classes were pushing for equal rights and wanted more independence. A female baccalauréat had been established in 1919, and Simone might well have been one of its beneficiaries. In a letter (not included in this publication) she mentions her 'little secretary', which indicates that she was not herself a secretary, and we can guess therefore that her job was reflective of her social background and education. Perhaps she worked part-time in some family-owned business, which would explain the free time and liberties she seems to enjoy.

4 It is worth noting that here Simone is referring to the telephone almost a century ago. At the time, Paris was one of the most modern cities in the world. The Paris Métro had been in operation since 1900, and the telephone had made its appearance before then. Charles Bonseul, the head telegrapher for the town of Douai, first revealed the principles of how it worked in an article called 'Electric transmission of speech', which appeared in *L'Illustration* in 1854. Granted, in 1928 the telephone was still the preserve of a small elite mostly from the aristocracy and the upper echelons of the bourgeoisie, but the city's first subscribers date back to 1881. Thousands of Parisians, then, had access to this means of communication which underwent important developments during the period

I must leave you, I shall quickly take this letter to the letter box. Goodbye, darling love. I am holding you in the wildest embrace!

Your Simone

---

of this love story, with the appearance in September '19 of the first automatic telephone exchange in Paris. From then on, subscribers had the iconic round-holed dial which meant they themselves could dial the alphanumeric codes: three letters followed by a number.

Proust mentions the telephone in his writing, particularly in *Le Côté de Guermantes*, in which he describes a conversation with his grandmother. When referring to telephone conversations in his correspondence, he often uses the charming neologism 'telephonage'. This gives us at least some idea of the circles in which our heroine lived, and although she is sparing with information about her social context, as confirmed by the quality of her writing and her style, there is no doubting she belongs to a privileged class.

My dear love,
    I would rather bring a smile to your face. I would rather be wrong but, on the other hand, what wonderful peace and quiet after such a day!

So you were utterly happy in my arms, and my embraces were not a disappointment. I am so thrilled, my loved one, because you know that first and foremost I want to please you.

I may have succeeded in giving you a delirious climax, but, believe me, mine left me powerless and quite drained of strength. The severe spanking you gave me has prepared me for the ordeal ahead. Step by step, I am climbing to ever crueller heights and one day, very soon I hope, I shall reach a place where you can at last achieve the perverse sensations you seek.

Yes, my darling treasure, you did suck me well. Oh, the deep-seated raptures that flood through me when you use your tongue and lips, and passionately kiss my excited little button! These wonderful ministrations which you manage to sustain for so long are what I anticipate most eagerly, for they are the apotheosis of all the passionate attention you lavish on me. But in your arms

I am always happy. I take pleasure nestling my head on your shoulder, and you wrap your arms around me so sweetly, pressing my skin to yours, that I wish I could spend hours like that, watching you sleep.

Darling Charles, I cannot write at greater length this morning for, alas, there are far too many things to stop me doing so, but I want you to know how very much you mean to me and how dearly I love all the things you do to me, even the cruellest.

Next time we meet I want to prove to you that I truly am prepared to suffer to make you happy, as that is your wish.

Delving into me with your eager tongue, bruising my buttocks with your impatient fingers, you were just as I remembered you when I was all alone back then. It really was with you that I was reunited, my dear darling lover. Did I pleasure you sweetly enough? Was it what you secretly wanted or were you disappointed? I do believe I felt a thrill of pleasure deep inside you when my tongue ventured softly, softly between the beautiful buttocks you offered up to me. Your cock strained and pulsated as my attentions grew more insistent.

And if you like the perverse ministrations I gave you, I shall always be happy to lavish them on you just as ardently. Yes, it really was exquisite feeling that impressive member while the whip strokes rained down on me. But next time, because you must never take me in a normal, ordinary coupling, I hope you will agree we should try that other way, and we can invent unexpected positions.

Oh no, we are still a long way from the limits of our fantasies. Till later, my dear darling. When can we make love to each other again, my dear darling?

With a gentle hug and frantic kisses on your lips and eyes.

Your Simone

D arling love,
    You shall drive me quite mad, do you hear, quite
mad with desire and pleasure. I did not receive your
pneumatique till this morning. I found it when I arrived
at the office. It only arrived at half past seven yesterday
when I had been waiting for it with such wild impatience!

I was violently overwhelmed with thoughts of you last
night in the warmth of this great bed which witnessed our
first couplings. I found the place where you lay your body,
I conjured you in my mind, so glorious in your masculine
nakedness. I closed my eyes, the better to relive our every
touch, and I was filled with furious longing for you, my
darling love. My whole maddened, fevered body contorted,
and I made the ecstasy of it last until my desire was simply
too strong. And then slowly, softly, savouring every ounce
of the boundless pleasure escalating inside me, I managed
to create the illusion I was in your arms and it was your
tongue stroking me lovingly. I had the wildest of climaxes
but, alas, the truth was that I was alone and you were so
close to me, barely a few yards away, but you had another
woman beside you, and were perhaps fondling her at that
very moment! Then I wept with longing, I called to you
softly, softly, your darling name stirring shivers of pleasure
which kept me awake for a long time on my solitary bed!

Dear love, do you realise just how much your body arouses me? Do you understand how utterly I am yours? I am your belonging, your very own thing, your toy which now lives only to satisfy your pleasures and perversions, and all of me is now but an echo of your passions. I do not know whether it is I who has instigated all your perverted desires, but as things stand now, nothing matters to me besides your body, your touch, your kisses. You have *all of me* to yourself, do you hear, my only reason to live is to be in your arms, experiencing the shocking ecstasies that bind me to you with an inviolable bond. The bond of wildest passion and perverse sensuality, and I now do not know whether I could ever bear for another man to touch me because the memory of your embraces is so exquisite. Beloved darling, do not inflict on me the appalling pain of breaking away from me yet. Tell me our love cannot end yet, and that when you are far from me in the place which snatches you from my embrace, you will manage to keep yourself for your mistress whose arms will open wide in anticipation of your return. Darling, I shall suffer horribly while you are away. My longing for you will grow more violent every evening, and I shall have to wait three long weeks before you take me again! I love you, darling love, do you know that? I am very afraid I no longer love you merely with my senses. My heart is also succumbing to the bewitching charms of your whole lovely person. I can tell because I am jealous of the hours stolen from me! Darling beloved, hurry Saturday so we can forget everything that is not us. Yes, we shall climb to new heights of perversion, but perversion is so wonderful! It is quite shocking being transported irresistibly towards release by such voluptuous delight. Darling, we can still dream up different ways of pleasuring each other, we shall strive to reach a pinnacle of pleasure together. Would you like that? Our bodies will mould closely together so that no ounce of our flesh misses out on the ultimate ecstasy.

Take me, take all of me. Come inside me. Be happy in my arms. I love you.

Simone

My dear darling,

I was so happy this morning when I received your little note, and more particularly very happy to know how much pleasure I gave you when we were last together. You see, my darling, I am always so afraid you will grow weary of my touch, that your need for me will soon be sated. A man's desire, even with the most loving of men, is a fragile thing and there is always that fear that it will flicker out like a flame in a gust of wind.

And yet, my dear love, I shall try to keep you as my own for as long as possible, for I am now so very accustomed to you that I cannot conceive of a separation. I feel that should you leave me, a great chasm of emptiness would open up around me and I would be sad, appallingly so.

You have succeeded in binding me to you with all the perverted charms of your caresses. Look how you proved what happiness you could afford me on Friday! I was happy in your arms, my dear beloved, so happy. Of course I suffered, but at least I could be sure that your pleasure outstripped my pain and, I hope you understand, this certainty would have seen me endure many more ordeals. And did you not reward me for my docile acceptance? Oh, the joy of feeling your pulsing cock probing into me! You skilfully kept me waiting for that exquisite moment, and your passionate attentions drove every inch of me wild as I cleaved helplessly to you. I wanted your flesh, but you surrendered your entire body to me. Did I succeed in making it thrill as you had hoped? I myself experienced the profoundest joy as I kissed every morsel of your flesh, even the most intimate parts.

My dear love, what a strong bond holds us to each other now! Our shared vices bring us closer together than any normal lovemaking which, I feel quite sure, would have given us both a sense of incompleteness, of unfulfilled pleasure. Don't you think we are happier like this, darling? The ardent sensations we experience together transport us to an other-worldly plane; we are gliding high above ordinary lovers who can never reach the extremes of pleasure that only couplings like ours can achieve.

My loved one, nothing can stop us now. Together we can scale the heights of madness, hand in hand, savouring every kind of forbidden embrace, let no pleasure remain unknown to us for that is how we love each other. I would like you to tell me all your thoughts, I should like to know if there is something else you want. Do you want to love me in a different way? Would you be happier if you could experience the normal kind of coupling with me?

Answer me, dear love. I love you.

My most intoxicating caresses all over you, wherever you want them.

Simone

M y darling love,
    If you only knew how happy I was to see you again! I wanted to take you in my arms, hold you deliriously to my heart that is so full of you, and passionately stroke every inch of your body which so tempts and lures me. Oh, the delicious vertiginous feeling that swept through me when your lips brushed over mine! I wished that kiss would never end . . . I was so frantic to see you again, my loved one, after such a long separation, and now we are to be separated once more. But before that we shall share many hours of madness because now you are utterly mine . . . When I saw you again I realised how very dear you are to me, and I know how ardently I shall caress your beloved body which stood so close to mine this morning that I could sense its every contour.

My love, you did not seem to notice that I was maddened with desire, but if only I had held you to me, what follies I would have committed! I would have kissed you frantically, your chest, your stomach, your thighs. I would have found your cock, so soft and warm. I would have taken it between my avid lips. I would have sucked him slowly, slowly, and felt him throb and grow in my mouth. Then I would have ventured lower and round the back, in the brown cleft between your charming buttocks, I would have found that sensitive place, and my tongue and lips would have given you all the caresses you so love. I would have tasted your most intimate flesh with such voluptuous delight, and I so regret that I cannot penetrate you as you penetrate me. I want to press my skin against yours, to roll my body on your palpitating flesh, leave no corner of your being virgin to my touch. I should like to invent good-ness knows what couplings to make you cry out with unsuspected pleasure, to harvest from your scorching lips words of erotic delirium, to watch you swoon with delight in my arms . . . Oh! Darling, I do so love you . . . Could you doubt it? You have sown such vices in my blood, and I now want the wildest of couplings, like no other. I love you, I love you like a rutting animal. I want to feel you penetrating my being, deep in my flesh. I want to come like a wild beast to your caresses or your blows. What does it matter to me? All I truly want is to love you, to love you, to give you pleasure with my fevered body which so wants to own you. My beloved lover, my little god, why are you not here to soothe this furious desire mounting ever higher, and driving me helplessly towards you? Hasten Saturday, I want to suffer, I want to love you. I shall suck you, and rub you, and love you . . . Oh, Charles! I am going quite mad with longing, I can bear it no longer. Every part of me aches as I cleave desperately to you. Till this evening, my loved one. I adore you. I love you. I want you.

Simone

My darling love,

I have read and reread your brief letter. How wonderful it was to have! I was so afraid I had disappointed you . . . Now I know that, though it may not have been perfect, you still experienced infinite pleasure thanks to that perverted touch. Yes, my loved one, next time you will have to have even more powerful climaxes, to have the illusion of being truly taken by a virile member piercing your flesh. It will probe you wildly in every direction, just the way you do when you take all of me in that same embrace.

Dear love, I was divinely happy in your arms. You left me quite powerless, my dear love, but oh, the intoxication I felt! Never before had I been so charmed by your caresses as I was then. Was it the spanking you gave me? Was it because your skin felt softer? I do not know . . . I cannot fathom what is happening to me, but I am happy in your arms, and I should hate to see that happiness come to an end.

I too shall be thinking of you in a few days' time, my love. In spite of everything, every last ounce of me will belong to you when you are far from me, and I shall relive all our hours of lovemaking in my thoughts. I shall draw on my memories for the patience required to wait for you like a good girl, but I do not believe I shall manage it for the memories are too sweet and too vivid. And so when I am in bed at night, before I go to sleep, I shall call my little god very softly. I shall close my eyes so that all I can see is his dear face.

Only a few more days of seeing you, and only so fleetingly. Do not forget me, my little god, think of all the tenderness you are leaving behind, remember I am waiting for you, that I want you with all the might of my senses which can only be appeased in your arms, by your touch. Promise me you will be a good boy over these long weeks, and that you will write to me *every day*, just as I shall to you. And if you really wanted to make me happy, but I mean really happy, well, you could have a photograph taken there and send it to me so that I could see my little god in his handsome uniform.[5] Would you do

---

5   The letters tell us that Charles was working in an office, yet two of them mention a photograph where he appears in uniform, suggesting that he is or was in the French army. Although the period of Simone and Charles's affair follows the Locarno Treaties and was characterised by an international policy of appeasement, the prospect of a new war was a constant fear in everyone's minds. The French army at the time was the biggest in the world and many young men were reservists, as Charles himself may have been, which would explain why he might still wear a uniform at times. The uniform remained an important symbol of manly prestige after the war, and Simone, as many other young women, would not have been insensitive to its appeal.

that for me? Would you? It is the only favour I ask of you until your return. For I know that after that I shall have every conceivable favour because you will bestow them on me with your caresses. They are the joy of my life, you know that. Goodbye, my dear darling. I am nestling against you to feel your soft skin against mine. I am planting silly kisses all over your body which I so love, and I am giving a long slow kiss to your beloved lips and your charming eyes whose gaze is so deliciously intoxicating.

Till tomorrow, my love, forget that I was unkind yesterday, but I was so afraid I had lost you. I love you. Your darling mistress.

Simone

Wednesday, midnight

I put off any explanations between us yet again this evening, Charles. I was too anxious and, besides, out on the street in those crowds, I just could not.

What has happened to you all of a sudden?

You must answer me very truthfully, my darling, with no reservations.

You have changed terribly in the last few days, Charles. While you were in Bandol your letters were more loving and tender than ever. Like me, you wrote unfailingly every single day, and your return to Paris was blessed with those unforgettable hours we spent together. But since then you have gradually broken away from me. You no longer even reply to my letters. I see you for a scant few minutes in the evening and even then you seem to be battling with invincible boredom while you are in my company. You are wilfully distant, indifferent to everything, and you seem only too eager to give me the swift goodbye kiss which will release you at last.

While I long for only one thing, for the moment when we can be properly reunited, you are already thinking of saying goodbye.

36

We mooted the possibility of seeing each other one evening this week, and I am still waiting to hear from you. I mentioned Saturday. You said you were leaving for the country.

This is all unfathomably painful for me, Charles.

Yesterday evening I thought you had something on your mind. I went for a walk around the Bois de Boulogne to calm my nerves. But, confronted with the same indifference again this evening, I cannot fail to notice the complete change that has come about in you. Which is why it would be best for us to explain things truthfully to each other and make everything clear. Why force our feelings? If I no longer have the appeal of novelty for you, we must not go on seeing each other, Charles. We must say farewell, kindly, while we still can. We must not delay. We must not risk compromising four months of perfect harmony with harsh words. We should go our separate ways just as we met, with a smile.

You see, there is no sense of heartbreak on my part in this letter, nor any wish to quarrel.

As ever, it is my heart and my deep feelings for you that dictate how I behave. Perhaps because, deep down, you do not know me well enough, you are hesitating to initiate a break-up. There is nothing to fear, Charles. Whatever happens, you will always be one of the finest memories of my life, and the time we have spent together and our excesses will always be uppermost in my mind.

But this evening I needed to tell you how terribly I am suffering. Because I *am* suffering, you must suspect that. Your letters from Bandol are still too recent for their exquisite words to have been erased from my mind.

And now I am writing to you from my bed, from our bed, by the wonderfully soft light of my little lamp. So, I cannot help it, I am casting my mind back over all our embraces, and feeling sad.

Oh, it does not matter, you know. It will pass. Don't go upsetting yourself. If it is over, well then, say so. I will be filled with sorrow, so much sorrow, so many regrets. Because I do love you, you know, I really do. But I shall not hold it against you. It is only normal, after all.

Goodbye, my little Charles, my dear, beautiful little god. Will you let me kiss all of your beloved body one last time? . . . that is what I wanted to do on Saturday, and will want to forever and ever.

I shall wait for some word from you, but if it troubles you, don't write. I shall understand.

My lips on yours in a deep, deep kiss.

Your mistress who loves you.

Simone

My love,

This is the last night I shall spend in this room.
I must move out of it tomorrow evening, and the very
thought of it fills me with great sadness. I feel as if I shall
leave some of my happiness and much of myself here.
You see, this evening a whole host of memories – more
even than usual – are swirling around me, and titillating
images are passing before my eyes. You are here, dear
love, right beside me. You undress in the small dressing
room. I can hear your every move. Soon you will appear,
magnificent and beautiful in your nakedness. This evening
the room looks just as it did on certain days. The small
night light on the chest of drawers casts its soft glow over
towards the big bed, and all around me, in vases in every
direction, the flowers I was given for my birthday yesterday
remind me of the red roses on that glorious July morning.

How I wish I were not alone in this great bed, my dear
love. If I could have you here, beside me, what follies we
could still commit.

When I left your arms yesterday my bruised body was
quite exhausted. Oh, the fury with which you beat me,
my loved one; my pleas did nothing to appease you, and

39

then your fingers clutched at my buttocks in a final spasm of desire. Today, dear love, I am a poor listless thing. Bearing the terrible marks of your passion. Do you know, you have so thoroughly whipped these buttocks you love that they are not a pretty sight now. They bear traces of the cruel whip that battered them mercilessly. Today they are just one huge bruise, and since yesterday I have been utterly drained by all our excesses.

But oh, how I love you, my little god! And how happy I am, for yesterday I knew you had tasted true rapture in my arms. When you looked at me your eyes were so alight, so full of victorious joy, and your kisses were so tender and so deep that, in your arms, I forgot all my pain.

My dear love, do tell me that I was a meek and submissive slave yesterday, tell me your cruel passion was sated and your delirious senses were appeased in victory. Was it good? – do tell me.

I wanted to prove how entirely I am yours. I had to undergo this ordeal, darling, so that you truly know that *nothing can separate us now*. If you doubted my love, if you were afraid I would give way, just look how much I love you, my loved one. Did I not tell you I was your slave? I have proved that I can suffer in order to make you happy. Come to me again this evening, my dear love. Come! This bed is too huge for us. It leaves us so much room because our bodies cleave so tightly to each other. Give me your lips, my loved one, my mouth longs avidly for your kisses. My inflamed senses can be assuaged only in your arms.

40

When I lie next to your skin, you feel unbearably sweet to me. Your flesh is irresistibly tempting. I want to press my lips to your body, I want to give passionate kisses to your thighs, to kiss your buttocks and your cock. And let me take my pleasure from you too; my desire is exacerbated just at the touch of you. I want to hold you close to me, to feel your skin against mine and when I am quite drunk on the wonder of you, when my lips have greedily had their fill, then you can take me in the wildest coupling, you can keep your desire simmering as long as you like, you can delve deep into my flesh with your hard rod. We shall both be intoxicated by our physical pleasure.

Charles, my dear love, I am frightened. I am sometimes afraid I love you too much. I live in constant terror of losing you. And I do suffer so when you are not with me.

I am losing my mind, Charles. I can feel my brain foundering. I now love you too much. I am hopelessly yours. I want to suffer more of your violent assaults because I know it is what you want, because I know that is how you perceive love. I love you with all your vices, all your passions, however perverted they may be. I want you, I have a furious longing for you. I am exhausted. Till tomorrow, my great love. Tell me we shall never part. Tell me you love me with all the power of your perversity. I should be so happy if you could write to me!!!

I love you, darling Charles.

Simone

M y darling love,
        I have just read your letter. What a lovely surprise and how happy it made me! At last I have found the same you I have known these last four months: a charming friend from the very first, and then an exquisite lover. I am happy, my darling friend, because I have succeeded in affording you many a pleasurable hour, and I ask only one thing, that that pleasure should continue as long as possible, for our love is truly a good thing, would not you agree, my beloved?

Yes of course the day will come when I allow you to perform the act you dream of performing. You will tie my wrists and ankles to the four corners of the bed and whip me furiously. I shan't be able to stifle my cries as the lash bites into me, and I know my supplications will not mollify you because you want to make my flesh suffer to the very last. But confronted with such a spectacle, you will feel desire stirring in your blood. Intent on the wildest excesses and with a feral glow in your eye, you will fuck me with helpless abandon, you will fuck my battered rump bearing the bleeding traces of your merciless lashing. What a glorious moment for you! You will have satisfied your passion, you will have assuaged the desire that has been haunting you, and you will take furious possession of me in the most passionate of couplings.

You are right, darling love, I did think of you yesterday evening as I do every day. But that solitary fondling does not appease my senses as fully as I would wish. I always miss your arms around me, my dear lover, and there is nothing to equal that feeling because you know so well how to pleasure me, how to take me, and the very touch of your young skin against my rump is enough to stir a most delicious intoxication in me.

I should like to take you like that, I should like my own flesh to pulse as yours does. Alas, I myself cannot give you this ultimate pleasure, and I must always resort to makeshift alternatives. But I should like to find an almost lifelike aid[6] so that I can watch you climax deliciously in my arms.

---

6 During this period there were no fewer than 224 registered brothels in Paris, each offering its own specialities for every social class. The luxurious Chabanais was famous for its illustrious clientele, such as the Prince of Wales, who had a special erotic chair that was kept at the institution to fulfil his fantasies. There were brothels for every taste; some recreated the atmosphere of a harem; some the courts of the Mughals; others the grandeur of Versailles or the gloom of a medieval dungeon. Many had special rooms for extreme fantasies, such as S&M practices. There was even a brothel for clergymen, the Abbey in rue Saint-Sulpice, while another, le Moulin Galant in rue de Fourcy, was reserved for the homeless. Le Moulin Galant was made up of two sections: the cheaper one was called the Deputies' Chamber and cost ten francs for five minutes, and

Darling love, I wish I could feel your tongue and your lips between my thighs again. I wish you would suck my button as you did on Saturday, for I have the most ardent memories of your attentions. It felt infinitely good coming like that, my dear darling, and I was also happy to swallow the best of you. What a deliciously titillating vision it was to see your cock's pink head extending further and further as I touched it with my lips. Had I dared, I would have frigged myself at the same time so we could come together, transported simultaneously by the same vertiginous voluptuous delight. But I was already spent. You had exhausted me, my love. Oh, do come home soon

---

the more expensive, the Senate, cost fifteen francs. Paris was indeed the city of unlimited pleasures, although its pleasure houses were regulated by the authorities; girls were submitted twice a week to a medical examination, a precaution that was far from being observed at the time in other major cities in the Western world. Simone would have had no difficulty in obtaining one of these 'aids' from one of these exclusive establishments, even though opening the door would have required some courage; clients were men only, and the women who would venture to the brothels were not usually of the highly educated classes. Simone would have felt out of place to be sure, although it's clear Simone did not lack audacity. I can hear her enquiring as to the materials the 'aid' was available in, perhaps ivory or Bakelite? Bakelite was one of the very first plastic materials and had just been invented, and was making its way into all art deco products of the time. Through the letters, we gather that Simone started with a reasonable-sized aid, and later became increasingly 'ambitious'. . .

from this trip so we can love each other passionately once more! I still thirst for your kisses and your touch, and your embraces alone can fully satisfy me. Everything else merely aggravates my desire, which means I am more and more in thrall to you.

Goodbye, my dear love. I shall see you later. I need to cover your mouth and eyes with the wildest kisses. I love you, my darling Charles. Never inflict on me the agony of leaving me. Please tell me how tenderly you still feel for me. And tell me all the wild excesses of your dreams. You now know that I am entirely yours and I shall always obey your every whim, however perverse it may be.

My darling love, I must go. I am nestling in your arms and watching you sleep, my little god.

Every inch of me is yours.

Your mistress who loves you so much.

Simone

My dear love,

Thank you for your long, chatty letter which I had been hoping for so eagerly. I needed to read your wildest thoughts to convince myself that you truly are happy in my arms. What makes you say I am demanding? Are you not demanding too, my loved one? If my letters are a pleasure to you, then you must see that yours are also a great joy to me.

Yes, my darling, I do apologise for going back on my word. I promised to bring the precious aid but, I so hope you will understand, I still felt unsure at the last moment. I am afraid I shall look so depraved, so perverse! And yet, I cannot explain the madness that makes me want to experience such sensations when I am with you. You make me happy, my dear darling, so happy. I have such delicious experiences in your arms, and now that my body has developed a taste for your attentions, it would not tolerate more chaste behaviour. You cannot imagine how I long for your touch. Feeling you naked against me, stroking every inch of me, stirring in you an imperious urge to take me, it all drives me wild, you know. Oh, the intoxication of watching your twitching cock gradually drawing up to his full height, taking him greedily between my lips, seeing the glow of pleasure that this special caress brings to your eyes. And then touching you in the other place, that is what you long for when you press up against me, yes it is what you are hoping for, darling, I know that now. I felt your whole body tense at the feel of my tongue, and when I drove my finger in deeper, a shudder of pleasure told me you were very close to climaxing. I wanted to create the illusion that I was no longer a woman, so I pushed myself hard up against your quivering buttocks and put my free arm around you, while my impatient finger probed your secret depths. Is that what you want? what you are hoping for? Are you forgetting my gender? Are you so perverse, my dear beloved, that you want to think of me as a man when your pleasure reaches its culmination? You are right, my loved one, being taken in that way is the most astonishing sensation, and I would not resent it if that were your secret desire. If I can give you the same pleasure, so much the better, and I find it arousing to think it is I who am taking you. I have devastating climaxes when I straddle you like a man. What would you like me to do to create an even more real illusion? Is there something I can add to what my own body has to offer for the sake of your pleasure? Tell me if there is. Be my guide. I shall follow blindly. No, we should not stop now. We are sliding a little deeper into depravity every day. Our perversion is leading us into the wildest fantasies. But which of us is complaining? We signed an unspoken pact from the first day we agreed to love each other. And, for now, nothing can break that pact but satiation. But we are not there yet, and we have many a pleasurable hour ahead.

Yes, if we are to love each other as we would wish to, we need a discreet little nest where nothing can interfere with our embraces. We need to shut ourselves off from the world so that we can be just 'us'. This winter we shall look for somewhere, would you like that? Because, alas, right now you are going away for such a very long time. Three long weeks without seeing you, without loving you. Oh, darling, it will feel such an age.

But when you return, if you still want me (you see, I didn't say if 'you love me'), you will find me impatient to be in your arms again, savouring your ardent attentions. If you like bruising my buttocks, then I shall offer them to you with no reservations or fear because now that I have suffered the whip, I am no longer so afraid of it and I know how much pleasure it gives you when I submit meekly.

My loved one, I am your dear little slave. Treat me as such but keep all your caresses for me forever and ever.

Do you know how fond I am of you, do you? Do you know how terribly I love you now?

My darling, my little god, you have such gentle eyes. Give me your lips too. It is such a delight, so sensual, lying in your arms, quivering to your touch, even when you are at your most brutal. Feeling you inside me, in my shuddering arse, as you probe it so ardently with your cock, is the most incredible sensation, it goes beyond anything I have known or could imagine.

Oh yes, I shall give you that sensation. I shall be the one taking from behind and you will come with such voluptuous delight.

I love you.

Till later, my loved one.

Your Simone

My darling love,
    I am sending you the long letter I promised.

First, though, I must thank you for the four long passionate pages you sent me on Friday. How can I describe all my joy when I prised open the envelope and found those ardent, tightly packed words? Of course I had been wanting a letter but could not have hoped for one so lengthy because, since Bandol, I have lost the habit of reading such missives from you.

When I tore myself away from you my whole being seemed to break in two. We were so close to each other on Friday! I could feel your whole adorable body throbbing against me, and your cock stiffening in my hand; oh, I would have taken you with such passion, my adored one. I had never felt every inch of me quiver so profoundly as it did then. I had the absurd notion that I might be leaving you forever. This thought flashed across my mind, and I held you to me passionately, pressing your lips as I imprisoned them with my own.

And for two days and two nights, my maddened mind and rutting body longed ardently to be back with you as you waited patiently for me.

And now I have just been in your arms, my lover whom I adore. I have come from your arms with no thoughts in my head and no strength left, but every ounce of me remembers and still shudders to the fire of your kisses. Oh, what a wonderful hour I have just spent with you! The door is barely closed before you reach out your arms to me and I bury myself in them, quivering all over with desire and love. Your mouth presses against mine in an endless kiss that intoxicates us both. Your hand slides slowly towards my thighs while I reach for your cock, which is already beginning to rear its proud head. At last you uncover the beloved little hole, and your wilful finger buggers me while I rub up and down your cock and reach for your balls to stroke them gently. With our lips still together, we stay there pressed against each other as our desire climbs to more imperious heights.

Oh, quickly, quickly . . . every minute is precious, my beloved, and I am so hungry for you, for every inch of your body which so haunts my nights alone.

Look, I am naked already, lying on the bed and waiting for you. Hurry, my beloved, come and join me.

But your much-loved body really is too tempting with its glorious soft white skin, and that straining cock stirs the wildest desire in me. I take it right into my mouth. I cannot suppress a groan of pleasure. Beneath my lips it gradually arches and grows fuller still. I am happy, my dear love, but you too now want to taste my pulsating flesh.

You press your mouth to my cunt. Your lips circle my button which jolts deliciously to this inflaming touch. Every inch of your flesh is close up to mine. Your mop

51

of brown hair disappears between my thighs, your stomach presses against mine. You brace your thighs on either side of my cunt. I still have your cock in my mouth, but your deliciously tempting brown balls are within reach of my lips. I shall attempt a still more unusual caress, one I have not dared try before. Very gently, my mouth draws in that warm flesh, and there between my lips, I feel one of your balls thrilling and quivering. My avid mouth smothers it with kisses, sucks in all of it, and my lips close around it. There it is inside my mouth, quivering like a little bird, and it is wonderfully delicious. Under the effects of this new ministration, your whole body shudders and thrills. It weighs more heavily on mine, we are now reduced to one being, tightly bound together. And for many a long minute, not relaxing our grip for a moment, we suck deliriously on each other's flesh, and our painfully ardent climax leaves us panting.

Oh, the love with which you lick this flesh, Charles. While your tongue carries out its devilish work, you bugger me with two fingers, and all I can feel is boundless intoxication. This orgy makes you groan with pleasure and I beg for mercy. How long is it before I do? No one could say.

I have no strength left, quite spent, but you are not yet satisfied and you drive the formidable rod[7] into my arse. There, my beloved, watch, watch. This is what I do

---

7 Translator's note: it's not entirely clear in the French, but she appears to be using the 'aid' here.

when I am alone and my longing for you is too powerful. The rod goes in and out, back and forth in my shimmering flesh. I'm fucking myself before your eyes. You slip one finger into my arse, then another, and I rub at my button while my tongue probes your hole, deep inside.

Could anyone dream of a more thorough orgy, a more perfect perversion and debauchery? We experience every pleasure, every climax together, gasping with sadistic[8] delight. These wonderful ministrations are making us lose our minds, and it is not over yet, oh no, it's not over yet.

My nails claw at your flesh but I am exhausted. You have emptied my mind and my cunt with your demonic embraces, administered with such perfect skill. Now I should like to watch my lover's body buck irresistibly in its final exploit. I want to watch him climax at last, right to the last drop, just as he did for me.

Your tensed fingers grip your cock. 'I'm tugging myself, darling, I'm tugging myself,' you say in a strangulated voice. Turn towards me. I don't want to miss a moment of this sadistic action. Your gorgeous eyes blaze with an ardent fire. You gaze briefly at your mistress's body still lying beneath you. You seem to be looking for a place to discharge your come. I'm ready, my beloved, ready to

---

8 Translator's note: this word was not as commonly known or used in the late 1920s and it may be that Simone meant it more as a reflection of extreme sexuality than the cruelty it has come to mean now.

receive this sacred baptism which will connect me forever to my lover's body. Tug it, tug at that magnificent cock stiffening beneath your fingers, tug again and again. I want to feast my eyes on this unique sight: performing the most perverse of gestures among all gestures, we are scaling yet new heights in our depravity. My lips and my arse have so often drawn your sperm out of you, but today it is you who will give it to me.

The first droplet beads at the end of your member. You close your hand still tighter; then I slip a headstrong finger between your buttocks and probe deep inside. A gasp, a cry, a shudder through your whole body and you ejaculate furiously, wildly over my breasts and my stomach. Your sperm jets out just as I wanted it to, abundant and hot, and my hand relishes in spreading it all over my body. I smother your cock with this beloved sperm. Oh, you made me so nice and wet, my darling, and I do love you so! I am happy, truly happy. I am yours forever, is that what you want?

My hopes have not been disappointed. We have committed our wild excesses just as we wanted to.

And you, my loved one, are you happy too? Did I meet your expectations? Did I succeed in bringing you to the most extreme of climaxes, just as you hoped I would?

Do you believe it would be possible to find embraces still rarer than ours? Would more sadistic passions be possible? Could even more thrilling delights be achieved, do you think?

I still have the traces of your kisses on my skin. I am exhausted by your absurdly skilful embraces. Tell me, who is it that teaches you such couplings, my most admirable of lovers?

How can I describe the joy of having your head between my thighs! Your lips pump out my come down to the last drop, because you suck me with such expertise that, despite the pain of so many successive climaxes, I do not have the will to tear your lips from my engorged button. If my touch makes you happy, I will lavish it on you with so much love, for there is no sweeter thing for me than feeling your flesh beneath my lips.

I shall think of you this evening. I shall look back over our excesses in my thoughts and dreams. I want to relive the ardent sensation of your sperm on my skin. It was unforgettable, and that perverse gesture of yours is engraved forever on my memory.

From now on when I think of you, I shall always picture you tugging your magnificent cock with an ardour matched only by my own as I contemplated that titillating tableau.

Tomorrow evening, if you can, I should like to have a long letter to read. I cannot wait to hear what you felt, my darling one, and I want you to tell me again if I brought you to a good climax.

Do you know how very tired I am? And I must end this letter, it is almost one o'clock.

Till tomorrow evening, my darling love.

I am smothering you with kisses as wild and mad as my love, all over you, everywhere. And if you want to make me happy, well then, press your expert tongue to my swollen button and make me climax helplessly, till I can no longer breathe. I shall take your adorable balls in my mouth and suck on them lovingly, not forgetting their handsome brother, your prick which I do so adore. Write soon, I love you, I am all yours.

Your filthy little Simone

Monday, midnight

My dear love,
    I was beastly to you today, truly beastly. Please forgive me but I was aggrieved this morning for I felt sure I would find a long letter from you when I arrived at the office. Not only did I receive nothing but then at noon you seemed cold and distant, and I was hurt, very hurt. My beloved love, were you disappointed by our last assignation? Did I not succeed in giving you every sensation your body craved? Did you leave my arms dissatisfied, having failed to sate all your secret desires? Yet I wanted to afford you every possible ecstasy. I tried with the lowly means available to me, to find a new form of pleasure for you. I believe it is this that failed to give you the profound experience you hoped to have. I myself, though, have cast my mind back over the scene and found I had to get up out of my seat, prey to a fever in all my senses with no lover's embrace to calm it. My darling friend, remember those moments we shared . . . You had barely finished undressing before you brought the whip down on my rump. Your blows lashed at my quaking flesh, which you then kissed. Your impatient lips delved around my brown hole which hoped for much better things, and I was

already filled with furious desire. Your hard cock strained towards me, and he too quivered with desire. He wanted my lips to caress him, to make his proud pink head swell further. He throbbed deliciously in my mouth, but we both wanted other things, your whole being craved the experience we had so often discussed . . . and the way you offered up your arse drove me to distraction. Now, the time had come for us to realise our demented dream, for you to feel as if you were being taken by a virile male member. With one finger I prepare the way, soon it will be followed by the aid (alas, a rather mediocre thing) which I have in my hand. Every inch of your most intimate flesh quivers in anticipation of this moment. I spread your buttocks but then I am not sure what happened. I am terribly afraid that you were appallingly disappointed. But my hand was on your cock, rubbing it up and down, and you were the one who signalled for me to stop. You were ready to take me. We were both carried away by a vertiginous climax. And later you made me so happy when you pressed your lips to my button. You sucked me exquisitely and afforded me the most exhilarating of sensations. And, my loved one, you ejaculated with your cock in my mouth.

What is it, darling Charles? Is it an illusion or am I right? Be frank with me, tell me the truth. Lies would be pointless between us . . . you know we have made no pledges to each other, and we are bound together only by our mutual pleasure. If my touch no longer has any appeal, if you now feel sated or even repulsed, tell me, my loved one, but stop inflicting the pain of seeing you so cold and distant. Telephone me tomorrow to tell me whether you would like to see me at noon or whether you would rather part on the farewell we said this morning.

I shall try to sleep with thoughts of you. I cannot promise to behave myself.

I press my lips to yours. I love you and smother you with frantic kisses. Till tomorrow, my darling.

Your Simone

My darling Charles,
    In among my mail this morning I found your *pneu* from yesterday delivered as a letter. You can imagine what I have been through since yesterday morning and the terrible night I have had. With no reply to my letter, I thought it was all over between us. So then, what could I do but suffer?

That is now in the past. I have heard your voice and my heart has pounded for joy. My dear little god, at last I know I still have you. The nightmare is now evaporating and giving way to the most exquisite of realities. But I really did suffer, you know. You will say it was my own fault. Perhaps, yes, but it was yours too because you have been so lacklustre when with me these last few evenings that I can be forgiven for thinking only boredom with our couplings could have this effect on you. Come now, let us forget it. I shall learn to know you better, the better to love you.

And yet I love you so much already and with such profound tenderness that I do not believe it possible for my feelings to be any stronger. I saw yesterday just how much you mean to me and how I miss your touch. I cannot wait, I really cannot wait to hold you passionately in my arms, to revel in the smell of your skin, to swoon under your penetrating kisses that have captivated all of me. My dear love, I want to spend many more impassioned hours by your side and, while I am under your spell, I want to forget all the sad, sad hours wasted on tears and anxiety. Make sure you have plenty of pleasures in store for me, I have missed them for so many days. Make me suffer your violent onslaughts. My skin wants to feel the bite of your whip, and when you hold me captive in your arms, when you have toyed with my body as your cruel passion sees fit, you will give me the wonderful reward that I long for with every ounce of me.

Darling Charles, it has been so many days since we were last in each other's arms! I am filled with the wildest craving for your whole body; my terror of losing you forever coupled with the boundless joy of being with you once more will propel me into your arms as a still more besotted mistress. I want to plant passionate kisses all over your enticing skin. I want to take your pulsing cock between my lips and tend to him until the best of you jets out. But what I want most of all is to take you again in that fierce embrace. I want to feel you shudder irresistibly. I want you to offer up your backside so my tongue and fingers can prepare your mysterious passage where my impatient 'member' will eventually venture and take all of you, giving you that wonderful sensation again, the sensation that I know you crave as intensely as I do.

My loved one, when you want me you will find me so ready to love you, and ready to suffer, because I know you will make me suffer to punish me for being so bad. The letter you wrote yesterday includes a threat which, should I not love you so much, would make me quake with fear. Beat me, darling, beat me, have your revenge. I belong to you, my whole body is yours. I am happy in your arms *because I adore you.* I am waiting for your telephone call. Could I come to you this evening? I cannot wait to see you and claim my forgiveness from your beloved lips. Give me your mouth, darling Charles, and then your eyes. I love you, do you know that? I want to keep you forever and ever.

Until this evening, my loved one.

Your Simone

My dear darling love,

What a wonderful hour I spent in your arms yesterday! It will remain engraved on my flesh and in my heart thanks to all the intoxication it brought me.

I was happy, so happy. I could feel my desire rising within me. You had that strange glow in your eye which fascinates and arouses me, and oh, the air of triumph when you bound my hands! I was quite breathless, anticipating my ordeal with all the strength of my love. I wanted not to disappoint you. Did I succeed, dear beloved? Of course, I suffered from the whipping, but then did I not feel your lips caressing my battered buttocks?

Dear love, do you believe it possible to live moments such as these still more intensely? I do not think it is. I believe we savour such exhilaration together that nothing could ever allow us to forget it. With our every assignation we become more bound to each other by our perversion. Every embrace ties us together a little more. The same desire keeps propelling us helplessly into each other's arms. Oh, may this tremendous joy last many a day more! May nothing ever separate us! It would be too painful for me.

I belong entirely to you, my dear darling lover, and I do not want to think of the terribly sad time when you will tire of me. Tell me you love me, Charles, and that you are happy in my arms. I want to hear you say it to reassure my heart. I kiss every last inch of you deliriously.

Simone

My adored beloved,

I was touched by your *pneu* which arrived yesterday evening just as I was leaving and had given up hope of receiving one. It made me doubly happy. You replied and your reply was as I had hoped. I adore you.

I am glad my letter was to your liking this time. I know what you like, my passionate love. Well then, listen:

I too want us to exchange the most outlandish of embraces. I want us to draw a maximum of pleasure from our bodies so we can never forget each other. Yes, darling, when we met the time before last, I realised that you wanted this new kind of coupling, and I told you how very aroused I was when I felt you slipping your warm cock so gently and tenderly between my moist lips. It felt indescribably good when you fucked my cunt. You succeeded in awakening in me a desire for this coupling which I had deliberately ruled out of our relations for many reasons. When next we meet, that is how you must take me, if you so wish, but you know what I expect of you if we are to lessen the banality of this coupling. You will be the one to drive the indefatigable aid into my arse. It will work such wonders in your expert hands, for you will know how to guide its infernal dance inside my brown flesh, and when you have quite giddied me with the delirious pleasure of it, then you shall take me, my loved one. You will penetrate me with your charming cock, you will fuck me passionately with all your fire and tenderness, and you will feel me shudder to a climax to make you believe you are having me for the first time. And so our love will be deliciously renewed. If we both have any strength left, I want you to be brutal and cruel. I want you to make me suffer with your merciless lashing, striping my skin with red weals. I will present my shameless rump to you, and you will bruise it with the full force of your furious passion. And when you have assuaged your longing for torture, you will kiss my fevered skin with your burning lips. Oh, darling, what wonderful delights our desire has in store for us! I am as impatient as you to experience them. Yes, my adored mistress, I shall be your male lover, and I hope my passion will afford you the most profound of pleasure. Give me your soft, soft body, I want to kiss it tenderly. I want to suck your cock, I want to suck your arse with my whole mouth, and take you imperiously with my impatient member. Spread your buttocks with your impatient hands. My tongue is opening up the mysterious passage, I hope you can feel it. I delve it as deep as I can inside you, giving you a foretaste of the coupling to come, which will leave you exhausted in my arms. Now I am pressing my stomach to your arse. Give yourself, give yourself. Can you feel the huge head poised before penetration? It goes up, and it goes down, all along your cleft. A thrust of my hips and I am buggering you passionately, my loved one. Is it good? Tell me, does it feel good?

Would you rather I pleasured myself in front of you? Well then, watch. See my finger coming and going between my wide-spread thighs. It skims over the button which stiffens to its exquisite touch. My stomach constricts with pleasure and later you can press your lips to me to harvest the abundant sap flowing from me. But I want you to do the same in time with me. I also want you to give me the titillating sight of your tugging yourself, and we can come together with the same intoxication.

This description is quite literally driving me wild, my dear love. I want to prove to you yet again how much I love you. I am so full of terrible vice, my beloved, and you are so very good at awakening my desire to perform the most perverse of couplings with you.

Do you believe we shall enjoy enough voluptuous pleasures when next we meet? But we shall need more time to ourselves because we are always in too much of a hurry.

I am already all aquiver at the very thought of these embraces. Whatever state shall I be in when I actually experience them in your arms?

Goodbye, my dear love. I send ardent kisses to every inch of your scrumptiously tempting flesh. I press my mouth to your lips in the deepest of kisses until very soon when I shall give you more and better things.

Do be good until then, so you have the strength to make me come the way we both want. I cannot wait to feel you in my cunt, taking sweet possession of me. What about you, do you want that too? Shall we now go against our own agreement? Never mind, I love you too much, but I know that your perversity will soon usher me back onto more forbidden paths. The most tender of kisses to you, my dear darling.

Simone

This previous letter marks an important turning point in the relationship: some six months after their meeting, the two lovers reverse genders, a change recorded not only in their acts but also in their words. Until now, Simone presented herself as a mistress who submitted to her partner's brutal fantasies and desires, succumbing not only to his blows but also on the question of 'normal couplings', something she had previously staunchly refused but for which she develops a liking.

But Charles's own taste for sodomy, which the increasingly bold Simone now no longer doubts, allows her to take a more prescriptive role in their relationship.

In this same letter she still calls herself his 'submissive slave', prepared to undergo his ever fiercer violence, but she also writes 'my adored mistress, I shall be your male lover'. She is not proposing or suggesting this, but declaring it. Simone, now more in love than ever, is taking proceedings into her own hands.

This is partly because she is increasingly afraid Charles will weary of her, so she feels she needs to take the initiative and stand her ground if she is to satisfy her lover's secret longings and, more importantly, to keep him.

M y dear love,
Do you know that today is an anniversary? Yes, it is already six months since we met. Six months since the first time we dared speak to each other after so many days when we both ardently longed to do so. Do you remember, darling? Do you recall sitting opposite me on the omnibus, the stolen glances, the eye contact full of promise between us? You were divine, you know, Charles darling. You were shy then. And I took such pleasure encouraging you by looking you in the eye throughout the journey.[9]

---

9 In *Illuminations*, Walter Benjamin quotes German sociologist, philosopher and critic Georg Simmel, who noted the importance of eye contact on newly available public transport: 'Before buses, railroads, and streetcars became fully established during the nineteenth century, people were never put in a position of having to stare at one another for minutes or even hours on end without exchanging a word.' Parisian culture, long influenced by a tradition of gallantry, was nevertheless characterised by a rare freedom and French women were well known throughout Europe for being loose and shameless in their eye contact. Henry Miller commented on this tendency in his novella *Quiet Days in Clichy*, where he describes an

Then one day you suddenly spoke to me. I replied with a pounding heart, and that was the beginning of our wonderful affair which has been such a delight these last six months.

My dear love, I wish I could have been with you today. I wish I could have intoxicated myself on your perverted kisses and arousing ministrations. The memory of our last assignation keeps me awake at night. I should like to experience those extraordinary sensations again, they have left me in quite a fluster.

But I shall have to wait a whole long week before I can hold you again.

Look, my beloved, I am hastily slipping off my clothes to join you on the bed where you are already lying naked, offering your buttocks up to my kisses. Let me glide my wilful tongue along the cleft. I can feel your brown flesh giving way to the pressure, and my tongue penetrates you, exploring and licking, while my hand softly strokes your balls and your straining cock. Not wanting to waste a moment, I rub my button which is swelling at this titillating sight. I reach a twofold climax, beloved, and sprinkle your thighs with the juices from my cunt. Ah, now it is your turn to press your tongue there, between my lips . . . Finish off your lucky mistress. Use your skilful

---

encounter with a lady in a cafe in 1930s Paris who held the gaze of any man who passed by; 'a French woman doesn't avert her glance as does the English or the American woman.'

kisses to make her swoon in your arms with voluptuous delight. Prepare her for the great battle your triumphal prick will wage on her later. He is readying himself now. Rearing threateningly over my mouth, soon to disappear right to the depths of my throat. A few licks of my tongue make the first drops of sperm bead on the end of this beloved prick, but it is here in me that he wants to discharge irrepressibly. You dive the 'other cock' boldly into my arse. Watch it coming and going between my buttocks, and I can already feel the pleasure of it wetting my lips. Take me, dear love, fuck me wildly. Probe it, go on, probe it while your hand tirelessly steers the other member's merry dance up my arse.

Oh, what an orgy, my love, what voluptuous shudders ripple up and down our bodies! Every inch of us thrills with perverted pleasure and we reach devastating climaxes with this double coupling.

There, my dear darling, that is how we shall spend our next hour of freedom after six months. Do you think we were made for each other? Do you believe we can still be happy?

Roll on next Saturday when we can put these follies into practice. I cannot wait to bury myself in your arms and feel the warmth of your skin against my body.

Giving you delirious kisses all over, wherever you want.

Your Simone

1929

My dear love,
 Why do you now so rarely write me letters like the one you gave me yesterday evening? Oh, the joy with which I read and reread it, and how my heart fluttered with happiness and longing . . .

I love you, I love you hopelessly and wildly, I love you with my heart, I love you with my body and my passionate senses. Whether near you or far from you, I am nothing but desire, and when I hold all of you in my arms, inhaling the intoxicating smell of your wonderful body, I wish I could secure them tightly around my treasure, my happiness, forever. As I write I am thinking of the touch of your lips, and I can feel rising within me all the ardent passion you have inspired in me, a passion that grows more enduring with every passing day.

Oh, my dear beloved lover, don't change. Stay as you are . . . Is your perversion not also mine? Has your passion not become mine? You have created me in your image[10]

---

10 Simone frequently refers to Charles as her little god, and at times uses biblical expressions, a tactic that speaks volumes about the pleasure she now takes in transgressing, even blaspheming. In spite of the separation between church and state in 1905, Catholicism remained extremely influential in French society. However, some families, especially in the capital's

and I have led you into the most salacious and voluptuous of couplings that my mind has invented to keep you. We are bound to each other, inexorably . . . we are just one body now, one body possessed by vice and pleasure, and it would take a Force more powerful than our Love to separate us now. Let's stay together, my loved one, let's hold each other close and our happiness can last as long as we want it to.

Like you, I can hardly wait till next we see each other. After a long, heartfelt kiss, the last of our clothing covering our bodies will fall to the floor one by one. When we are both naked, fired by the same passion, we shall race into each other's arms and the contact of our feverish skin will make us shudder deliciously. What sweeter moment is there, my loved one, than when you open your arms to me? When I stand against you, I can feel your skin next to mine. Our lips meet and my tongue finds yours in an intoxicating kiss . . . Oh, come to me, come to me quickly; the minutes tick by . . . Crush me with the weight of your whole body, on my body . . .

And the celebrations begin. The celebrations of our

---

intellectual circles, would not go to church at all and might actually go as far as to declare themselves atheist. Through close reading of Simone's vocabulary, we can surmise that she received a Christian education, as the overwhelming majority of French people at the time did, but possibly at this point in her life she was not concerned with the precepts of her religion. She will, however, come back to God later, as the other correspondence found in the briefcase reveals.

rutting senses . . . We are to climb to another new level today. To do something we have never yet dared do. I lie on my back gazing at your nakedness. Your opalescent skin there before me. Oh, how beautiful you are, my little god.

Take your cock in your hand. I'm watching . . . And I take the other member too, I drive it into my cunt and fuck myself before your eyes. Tug yourself, my love. Your prick is already growing to the touch of your hand. I can see his pink head emerging from between your clenched fingers. While I fuck myself I stroke your arse with my other hand. With one finger I probe your most intimate flesh, and can feel it contracting. What a sight, my beloved! You are watching your mistress fucking herself and I am watching my lover tugging himself . . . Oh, your prick is so beautiful! How wonderfully it will ejaculate! But your eyes are losing focus, your pleasure is escalating. I draw out the member slick with my juices and plant it deep into your frenzied arse. Now that you have been taken, you can resist no longer and there before my eyes, arching above my body which is swooning in ecstasy, you climax furiously. A warm gush flows onto my smooth stomach. Give me all your sperm, my loved one. Not one drop must stay in your prick, I want to harvest all of it on my body, and I shall spread it over my breasts and my stomach because I want to feel its intoxicating warmth all over. Then I shall be more yours than ever; I shall be yours thanks to this perverted gesture we have shared. Who but us would dare do it?

And then, at the touch of your lips, you shall feel the juices flowing from my cunt, for I too shall climax wildly, my loved one. You will gather my warm come and I shall taste its bitter tang on your lips . . .

If we both have enough strength left after this orgy, you will take me in a gentle coupling. You put such sweet tenderness into fucking me that you have reawakened my longing for this form of embrace. And we are allowed it, for it is a consecration of our lovemaking. We embellish it with so many perverse touches that it too becomes perverted. Oh, quickly, roll on the end of this curse which is depriving me of your shameless ministrations. I cannot wait to be with you again, my passionate violent lover, I cannot wait to have you in my arms to intoxicate you with my kisses. Yes, your body is mine, I do believe you now, and I am happy. I shall take you with such abandon, for I love you more than anything in the world.

Yes, I want to use my shameless attentions to make you come to the very limits of your strength. You are mine now, do you know that? And soon you shall be even more so, when you have wetted me with your sperm. Every inch of my body will taste this supreme sap, and you will see this wildest of moments in your dreams: your mistress groaning with pleasure under the jetting of your prick as it strains over her body in the final jolt of ejaculation.

Oh yes, be mine, and mine alone, my beloved god. Say those intoxicating words again. Drive away the contempt-ible pain of jealousy which grips me at the very thought that you belong to another. Tell me that you prefer the touch of *my* hands. Tell me that you are merely passive in *her* arms, and that I alone know how to give your inflamed senses the voluptuous rewards they crave. I want to love you still more ardently . . .

It is gone noon, I am afraid I shall have to stop. Till Monday evening, darling love. Write me a long letter like yesterday's.

I am kissing every corner of your beloved body, your lips and your wonderful eyes. I am entirely yours.

Simone

Now stiff and with sperm quite filled,
Your prick, pleasured by a hand so skilled,
Strains his head towards my backside
And gently over my flesh does glide.

Having hovered briefly and having teased
The hole that longed only to be appeased,
All at once it drives deep into the place
That welcomes it with passionate grace.

Now deep inside where you ravish me best
I can feel the ardour of your cock so blessed.
And under the effects of this perverse embrace,
I climax, and read in the joy on your face

The pleasure afforded by spilling the slick
Sap that filled your glorious dick.
And with one last breathless shiver
You collapse onto me all aquiver.

Bugger me now and let us come together.
Make me climax again, now and forever,
With this coupling that many a lover may shun
Which leaves you happy, exhausted, undone.

To keep the flames of your ardour fanned,
I reach between my thighs a shameless hand
And pleasure myself for your eager eye to see,
Then shower your mouth with the best of me.

March 1929[11]

---

11 French culture places a high value on all kinds of poetry. An educated person in the 1920s could of course compose sonnets and other forms with rhyming lines. School education heavily emphasised the importance of a good knowledge of classical literature, so that anyone who had gone to secondary school was (and still is, though to a lesser extent) capable of quoting numerous verses by seventeenth-century poets, such as Racine, Corneille and Molière. Simone's poetic skill, although used here for 'naughty' reasons, demonstrates her cultural background and familiarity with the great tradition of French poetry.

My sweet love,
   I have finally managed to get away from today's outing. I am the keeper of the treasure and no one yet knows why I am so keen to stay here. Let them have the great outdoors . . . My Charles, I just could not wait to be alone here with you, to come and tell you how tender my feelings for you are.

I have your little photograph before me now. You look out at me wisely with those gorgeous eyes, and your beloved mouth seems to be suppressing a mocking smile. I do so love you, my faraway little god, and I kneel at your feet to adore you with all the fervour of my love.

Two days already, two interminable days without seeing you, without reading your words, without hearing your captivating voice. I am so sad when I am far from you, my dear beloved, and oh how my heart is counting the hours until I can next feel your touch and your kisses!

Alas, there is still a whole long week to go before you come back to me, before I can hold you in my arms. And how many days will we have to wait before we can savour our magnificent couplings again? But at least you will be here beside me and I shall have the strength to contain my impatience for as long as I have to. But when we are far apart, my craving is exasperated. All our impassioned exchanges come crowding into my mind, arousing me with no hope of appeasement. No, far from your arms, far from your much loved and much longed-for body, I cannot be happy. I miss you immeasurably, my sweet darling, and I am only sad I cannot prove it to you.

I am picturing you now completely naked, lying on your back with your thighs raised to reveal your little brown hole as you offer it up to my ardent kisses. Your hardened cock thrills to the touch of my hot lips but my attentions are not focused on him. Oh no, it is your buttocks I want, your beautiful firm buttocks. I want to drive my impatient tongue between them, and press my avid mouth to your hole . . . Go on, please, let me, let me. Ah, my sweet love, it is so good sucking on this flesh, and what could be more arousing sight than a lover's adored body quivering with pleasure under the effects of these skilful kisses?

That is what I think of when I am far from you. That is what I crave, and your absence is painful. Oh, if I could be with you, my sweet little Charlotte, I should be so happy! Why did you not take me with you the other evening? Why did we not set off together towards oblivion, towards the joys of total possession, even if only for a couple of days? Oh, Lottie, to have you to myself, far from anyone else, for a whole night . . . what an extravagant dream!

Come back soon, my loved one, for alas we never have more than an hour together . . . Come back, so that we may be quite inexorably together for that one hour. I need your adorable body more than ever, and I want your arms around me, your wild kisses, your brutal, indomitable couplings which leave me exhausted, which hurt me but also drown me in the depths of voluptuous pleasure!

And do you, like me, long for these salacious acts? Do you want to savour new vices in my arms? Have I succeeded in giving you unforgettable experiences? Are you happy with me? Tell me . . .

Shall I have a long letter from you tomorrow? I am horribly impatient and today will now feel interminably long! And how will you write to me? With your heart or with your perversions? What words will your body's cravings have dictated to you? Tomorrow shall I find one of those entrancing letters like those you wrote to me from your little room in Bandol six months ago? My dear love, I am afraid you are less passionate now. To think we are almost old lovers! Ten months, and counting, and is your desire any less pressing? Have you tired of me?

No, darling Lottie, no, don't tire of me . . . We have not exhausted our strength, and when you return we shall love each other so wildly that your lust for perverted excesses will blossom again to my kisses.

I hope you will be able to write to me again, up until Thursday, until you leave for Nantes. I shall be so appallingly unhappy all these evenings that lie ahead. I shall come home all alone, without you. And we have only a few days left to come here together, after that there is a four-month separation . . .

Goodbye, my great love. Do be good and think of me . . . I hope you have fine weather, as we do here, and that your brother and his family are all well.

Holding you tightly in my arms and taking your beloved lips in a long slow kiss from the bottom of my heart which is so full of you.

I adore you and my whole life is now spent waiting for your return . . .

With passionate kisses on your two hands,

Your Simone

Darling beloved,
     A week ago now I had only just left your loving arms, quite drained by your exhausting attentions; you had spent a whole hour bending my body to suit your every whim, your every vice, and my whole being still thrilled with all the pleasure you had kindled in me. Oh, how expertly you made love to me, my dear love!

Alas, this week I must be good despite all the longing I feel, all my longing for your adorable body which I should like to treat to a thousand ministrations. Your body that I should like to savour at every minute, every second, enjoying the rousing taste of it that sets my nerves on edge with insatiable desire. The more I have you, the more I love you. Far from wearying of the treasure chest that is your body, I only love it more. With every assignation you grant me, I find yet another reason to love you, and I leave you with an ever more pressing need for your kisses and your hands on me. When we are apart I think of the excesses we have just enjoyed together, and all our wonderful, powerful shared memories rise up to the surface of my heart. They unsettle its state of calm, they make it beat faster and I eventually fall asleep with my head ablaze and my limbs heavy, infuriated by so much pointless ardour which you are not there to appease with a kiss.

Oh, I do love you, my dear one, I love you with such an extravagant, all-embracing love. I love you in a way I shall probably never be able to again, once I no longer mean anything to you. I have given you my whole life, my body, my heart, my thoughts, all of myself in fact, and I can tell I shall never take them back. Whatever happens to a love like this, whether you keep or break it, you shall be locked into my heart forever in all your seduction, all your charm and all your perversity. You will be the one and only lover for me, the one who can only ever be loved once, the one who reveals my true self to me. For a long time, perhaps forever, I shall feel the warmth of your touch deep in my flesh, and I shall always be yours, yours, yours.

Oh, my love, how I love you, how I hunger for you, for your adorable body. The memory of it haunts me constantly, irrepressibly. I love your girlish young flesh, so soft to the touch, so warm against my cheek. I love your little pink nipples and your virgin breasts where my mouth comes to rest. And your pale, taut stomach, and the brown curls between your thighs, the pretty flower of your pink cock with its mysterious hole, a soft nest in which my tongue can nestle. Oh, I shall soon have it, I shall have all of this body, won't I, my love, in just a few days! We shall meet in our room and I shall have all these treasures entirely to myself. My whole life is now spent waiting for the moment when you surrender yourself to me with all the shameless abandon dictated by our passion. You appear before me in the dazzling splendour of your nakedness, and my lips seek out the place where the kisses will do their best to arouse this flesh so willingly offered to them. And I know where that place is, I guessed where it was almost on the very first day. My love made me perceptive and I had not a moment's hesitation in directing my tongue towards your adorable arse. Oh yes, that truly is the best place for an arousing kiss, isn't it? Give it to me quickly, darling treasure. Ah, how I love it, and I kiss it tirelessly while my fingers pleasure your cock. And to ensure my victory is complete, I bugger you furiously. You belong to me, you are my plaything and I want to keep you forever and ever.

In a few days you will see my hands holding that monstrous tool which conquered your flesh. And that shocking sight put me in a quite demented state. Whatever will it be like, then, when I have an impressive dildo strapped around me, with its full balls smacking against your buttocks?

You will stay in the same position and, in order to hold you firm, I shall grasp your hips; I shall pin you down with my arms so you cannot escape the terrifying coupling I shall inflict on you.

I shall be truly happy when that day comes, darling beloved, and my wildest wishes will have come true. I live in eager anticipation of the moment when I shall become your lover, *your man*. Yes, I want to be your man just as you are my mistress. I want to give you the same pleasures you give me when your pink tongue tickles my cunt's pink button. Oh, Lottie, how expertly you get my juices spilling from me! Do you know, I am now filled with furious desire to be fucked, to feel my lover probing deep inside me to release waves of come. Yes, you should feel proud because you have taught me to love that coupling so much that I could not bear to be without it now. We are all square: I bugger you, you fuck me and we shall always keep it that way, shall we not, my loved one, united by our shared vices and our all-powerful passion?

Next week I expect we shall be able to love each other with our usual abandon. Our bodies will seek each other out in the half-light, our mouths will meet in end-less kisses and our most intimate parts will be lost in each other in the most wonderful of couplings. I adore your sweet little breasts, they are the breasts of my imaginary mistress. They are charming, delicate little toys I can hold in the crook of my hand. Let me linger on them for a while. And you, my dear treasure, you will delve your impatient tongue through the secret folds of my cunt. I shall feel your warm breath on my engorged button and you will drink up the waves of juices released by your kisses. And you will kiss my nipples too. Do you know how I adore it when you do that? Darling, I cannot think of everything we might do but I am sure we shall commit great follies, shan't we, my loved one, for what could we do together but commit follies?

More than ever now I want to be 'your darling slut' so you can find every pleasure in my arms. And you will be truly filthy with me so you can match up to your mistress, won't you, dear love?

What will you do, dear friend, when you have me beside you? Tell me quickly what you want of me when next we meet.

Oh, I cannot wait to take you in my arms and press my body up to yours to see the dark flame of desire light in your eyes. I like watching your desire escalating in sudden waves. It soon submerges you and you cannot fight the sheer strength of your blood beating violently in your veins. And you take me in an endless coupling which breaks me in two, bends me to your will and makes me shudder irresistibly. Yes, I am yours, do you know that, darling love? And do you want to keep me forever? Are you mine forever, my lover whom I adore?

You say I am the one who has made you the perverted creature you now are, I am the one gradually dragging you down the slippery slope of all-encompassing vice. Perhaps, but surely you too have instilled in me this craving for ever more pleasure, you have made me seek out peculiar and unsuspected ministrations. So, you see, our love was born of a meeting of minds, born of the thrill when our eyes met, and of the way our bodies called to each other. We came within touching distance of each other for days and days, and we both had the same intention, we both knew we must persevere, that happiness was there, in the fusion of our two beings. We gave ourselves before we even knew each other, and what came next proved we were right. Since becoming lovers, we have only ever known pleasure together, and the way we give ourselves and take each other affords us boundless ecstasy. Yes, let's keep it to the two of us, my dear love, just the two of us. If you want to, we could try this idea which has become an obsession for us both, but I do not believe it will give us any greater voluptuous delights than our own ever more ardently pleasurable couplings.

Goodbye, dear love. Shall I find a long letter from you when I arrive on Monday morning? I do hope so. And now I shall say 'see you soon', for I hope we shall be making love in a few short days.

I adore you. My mouth wherever you want it. Just tell me, where?

Simone

My loved one,
What an entrancing letter, and how aroused I still am by it! Even though I have reread those passionate words again and again since yesterday. And how much more I love you, my dear love, when you give free rein to your heart over the pages.

Darling, you asked me whether, like you, I remember our first lovemaking. How could you think that such a memory is not locked in my heart forever? Charles, could I ever forget that, thanks to you, it was in the course of that morning that I had my first glimpse of true pleasure? Of course the scene is still very clear in my mind's eye, and I never think of it without a little shudder of happiness. The way we moved, our shy words, our first awkward caresses, the very first time we were in each other's arms . . . all of it is deeply embedded in me. But how unlike our true selves we were then! And how we both hesitated to explore the violence we could feel hovering just beneath the surface. Yes, I remember, dear love. The near darkness in that discreet bedroom hid our mutual embarrassment. On that soft double bed our naked bodies sought each other out and discovered each other. Our languid limbs tangled clumsily, and a vague feeling of disappointment after our first contact during the first rendezvous (do you remember, darling, the lovemaking that almost did not happen?!) meant we were hesitant about trying again. But you then took the offensive, my darling, and your violent desire lit an unfamiliar flame in your eye. You were so beautiful that morning, so ready to violate the body you were being offered! You suddenly threw yourself on me. Your fingers left their imprint on my rump which glowed red from your spanking, and before I even had time to understand your bold initiative, with one irresistible thrust you bore into me, bruising my most intimate parts. And we soon collapsed exhausted in each other's arms. Now at last we knew we had an understanding, for we had the same perversion and shared the same immeasurable pleasure. My darling love, it will soon be a year since I became your mistress and not once since that happy day have I failed to experience the most unforgettable sensations in your arms. And so you see, I love you more with each passing day, and I shall always love you with the same fervour, the same steadfastness, for as long as you wish it. When I am in your arms, my beloved, there is only one thing I want, and that is to do what you want, and I have only one desire, the desire to go to the very depths of your being to kindle your pleasure. I want to take you ever more fiercely so that, for that one hour, you are utterly mine, so that you cannot escape and so you leave my arms exhausted, powerless, and incapable of giving your body to the Other Woman later that day. Yes, my loved one, that is how I love you, with an exclusive love which suffers from the need to share. I want you to climax passionately in my arms so not a drop of the best of you should go anywhere but inside me that day. And when I am by your side I always want to push us to the very limits of our strength, for I know the happiness such exhaustion can bring.

And, dear loved one, that is how it will be on Monday. I shall give you the perverse sensation you so love once more. With the full force of my own depravity I will steer you to the very pinnacle of exhilaration. You will quite unreservedly surrender to me the treasures of your beloved body and, like a passionate lover spurred on by the beauty of his mistress, I shall kneel before you and offer you my every desire with my kisses. I shall wrap you in the infinite tenderness of my heart, and before intoxicating myself on your warm, firm flesh, I shall lull you almost to sleep with my lascivious stroking which will see you drift into a half-sleeping state, and you will be woken when my triumphant member takes possession of your innermost flesh. You will be woken when your pleasure explodes as suddenly and unexpectedly as rain from a storm cloud. You will feel first pain, and then pleasure. And you will collapse a passionately happy man onto my panting body, quite spent after such a coupling. Yes, my one and only love, my dear lover whom I adore, I shall violate your magnificent body just as you once violated mine. But, in order to spare you the searing pain of this rape, my penetrating kisses will prepare the way for my superhuman member. My soft, skilful tongue will glide slowly into that little brown hole. It will keep it prisoner between its lips for a long time, and when the hole has softened, then your darling perverted Simone, your filthy passionate mistress, will press her demented, thrilling flesh against yours. In all the delirium of her rutting senses you will become her 'mistress' and she your 'man'. You see, my darling, our cravings are indistinguishable from each other. You dreamt of a vigorous male violating your flesh. While I dreamt of a gentle, lascivious mistress. Our extraordinary love has achieved the miracle. As our passions dictate, we shall take turns, changing sex and therefore achieving double the pleasure, double the ecstasy. Ah, Charles, how I bless the day fate brought us together! How I bless your audacity and my weakness! To think I almost fled when you became more insistent. Did I have enough of an inner struggle before sinning? (Yes, that was how I saw it then.) But, can you see, we were destined for each other. Did you espy the passionate lover in me? Tell me, did you suspect all my depravity? Oh, I love you, I love you so frantically, darling.

Yes, my little god, you will succeed in intoxicating me with your touch. You know you will. Surely you remember the moans of pleasure I could not suppress when you sucked passionately at my little cunt? Well, you will embark on that task again. You will make me die of pleasure with your skilled kisses. Yes, darling, suck me, suck me. You are so good at it. Suck up the very last drop of my bitter come and drive your hard prick into me. Stay there without moving, and when your prick is truly covered in that abundant sap, I can lick it dementedly. I can taste my own juices on your member. Neither of us knows what we may do next. Or perhaps I shall make a necklace for your cock with my breasts, or with my eager mouth, taking in every inch of him. Unless, despite how very foolhardy[12] this would be, I choose to feel him drive into my shuddering cunt and to hold you to my breast so that our bodies become indistinguishable in our close embrace. Oh, darling, I want to be unreservedly yours, to belong to you, to you. I want never to tear my body from your voluptuous body. I want to sink into ever deeper delights thanks to your touch. What an exquisite dream! Yes, loved one, I love you so much I throw all caution to the wind. I love you so much I shall give you

---

12 There is no doubt that Simone's use of 'foolhardy' here is in reference to vaginal penetration, and indicates a real concern about pregnancy. The main contraceptive method at the time was condoms, which when first used in the Middle Ages were made of animal bowels, until fabric condoms were invented during the Renaissance. Rubber condoms became available in 1928, followed by liquid latex condoms in 1930, the year in which the love affair ends. Contraceptive coils were available, but did not seem to allow full satisfaction. Abortion methods were still very primitive and dangerous, mainly involving knitting needles which caused infections and frequent deaths. Simone's concerns, therefore, are by no means futile.

every part of myself if you insist on it. If you want to take me in a different coupling, if you want your cock to take shelter in a softer haven, if in fact you now want to savour the normal kind of lovemaking that we have banned, I feel I could not refuse you anything, nothing, not even that. Tell me, do want this of me, for me to give myself to you so completely? Do you want me to open this hitherto closed door to you? Do you want to possess me fully, in the normal way? I want it if it will afford you new pleasure.

On Monday we shall belong to each other again. On Monday, my loved one, we can love each other passionately with the equipment at our disposal, until we have something better. I am entirely yours. I am your darling slave. Take my body whichever way you want, I am yours.

Goodbye, my loved one, till tomorrow. I am kissing you passionately all over your adorable body and nestling in your arms to savour the full sweetness of your exquisite attentions.

All of me is yours.

Simone

Here Simone reveals to us an invaluable detail about her personality: up to this point readers might have construed that she was quite devoid of restraint or morals. We now see that she actually struggled before allowing her passions to express themselves so fully. When in an earlier letter she mooted the possibility of using an 'aid', she mentioned her fear that Charles might find her depraved and perverted. And she uses vocabulary associated with society ladies of her day ('sinning'), although she mitigates this with her 'Yes, that was how I saw it'. But none of this prevents her revealing her Sapphic proclivities. So it is not that Simone had no boundaries, only that she took great pleasure in breaking them.

My darling little Lottie,

I dreamt of you very vividly last night. But why? Is it that I so regret not holding you in my arms this last week? Is it the sadness of not seeing you for two days? I cannot know. But in my dreams I lived the wildest ecstasies, and this morning I find I am still reeling from the violence of it.

But oh, how I prefer the living reality to my dream, however sweet it may have been. I shall never forget our last assignation. I discovered in you the passionate mistress I had long dreamt of finding, you even went beyond my hopes. For I must confess, darling Lottie, that is another of my vices.

In you, though, I found a twofold creature: a wonderful lover and a heavenly mistress. And I am filled with boundless happiness when I think of the last hour we spent together. I finally had you back in my arms after so many days' absence. I planted fervent kisses all over your soft skin and, as we were both overwhelmed by an ardent longing for perverse release, you slid underneath me. There I was, on top of you, imprisoning you with my body, with my stomach pressed up to you. Oh, the madness that gripped us both then! I had become a passionate man and you, my darling Lottie, the filthiest mistress anyone could ever imagine. I could feel your entire body quivering beneath me. You reached for the triumphant ramrod, offering yourself towards my rigid member. In a series of voluptuous spasms you gave me all of yourself. Every expert flick of your hips answered my own movements. I fucked you wildly and you yourself anticipated my every thrust. For a few moments I really felt that I was the man and you the woman.

In my madness, our roles were reversed and I had the most adorable of mistresses in my arms. Oh, Charles, surely you too want to experience that again? Surely you want to intoxicate yourself with such excesses? Do you not have ardent memories of that unique hour among all hours? Do you not want to reveal yourself as an indefatigable mistress, as you did then? Yes, Lottie, that is how I should always like to love you.

I should like to locate the precious aid we still need. I should like to take you like that with a huge prick strapped to me. Your arse would not offer itself up to my stomach in vain, for with every thrust of the hips you would feel my cock driving deeper inside you, and you could then truly believe that I was your lover.

My little Lottie, do try to free yourself for an hour this week. On Saturday . . . and come to me, come so I can fuck you passionately. I need your adorable body more than ever. Goodbye, my darling love. Do not leave me with no news until Friday. I am sad when you are away from me; oh, my love, I love you so much. If you have not tired of me, come quickly. We can sink once more into a sea of vice, our omnipotent master.

Think back over our wild behaviour and remember I am filled with an ardent desire for every inch of you, my adorable mistress. My every moment is spent longing for the magical gift of your arousing body, and I cannot wait to whisper in your ear all the passionate words dictated to me by my passion.

Goodbye, adorable Lottie. Telephone me whenever you like. I am waiting impatiently for news of you, beloved little mistress.

Holding you in my arms and kissing your delicious little arse with my whole mouth.

My mouth on your lips in the wildest of kisses.

Your Simone

My darling treasure,

How can I describe my delight last night when you took from your pocket the long letter I had given up hope of receiving! I needed those passionate words to intoxicate me still further, darling Lottie, and I am happy this morning.

I have read it many times and every sentence feels like a sweet caress to me. Oh, how I love you, my Charles! How could you fear I shall weary of you some day? Do you not know your own power, my beloved, do you not know how utterly I am yours, and will be forever? For even if we are to part one day, my body will never forget yours and will always bear the indelible imprint of your love.

Yes, darling friend, I have become filthy and depraved and I should like to be even more so to thrill you and keep you in my arms. I want to see your eyes swoon thanks to our orgiastic embraces, I want to see you maddened with perverted desire, throwing yourself on me, bruising my flesh, biting and scratching these buttocks you so love. I want to see you like a rutting animal taking this body that belongs to you.

My love, I too dream of a discreet love nest where we might at last be cut off from the world and might give free rein to our mutual vices. I can picture my naked body. I see my arms and legs tied to the four corners of the bed, with a fine rope tight around my wrists and ankles. My rump is offered up, as if taunting you. You too are naked, in all your splendour, and with your eyes clouded by desire, you press your lips to mine in a kiss that comes from your very soul. Ignited by this fiery kiss, I too shudder with longing, a longing for your body, but you want to make me suffer. You gently stroke my naked rump, following every contour. The exquisite feel of it makes my skin tingle and thrill. All at once a hideous whistling breaks the silence in the room. A cry, a victorious cry; another cry, a cry of pain. The whip leaves its red mark on my skin. Another lash and then another. I struggle in vain, I plead. My rump writhes desperately to escape the whip but still it comes, tirelessly. And you, my beloved, you stand there enjoying the suffering. I can see your stiff prick, your glazed eyes, your air of triumph. You so enjoy this victory, but taking pity, you untie the cords which hold me prisoner and free this defenceless body, it has suffered enough.

And now I am lying on the bed, pale and drained. My buttocks are smarting and red. Come and soothe them with a gentle hand. Bring your beloved lips to this wounded skin and, with your kisses, make me forget the painful ordeal your cruel perversion has inflicted on me.

Stroke every inch of this body, it is yours. Run your hands down my entire length. As they travel down, stroke my breasts, my stomach and my thighs, and then slip between my legs and, below the dark curls, press your moist lips to my stiffened button which longs for your kiss. Oh, what a wonderful moment! A ring of warmth around my button. Your skilful tongue reaches and probes and licks my most intimate flesh. Yes, there, loved one, there. Take this button between your lips as you would a hard cock. Again, again, go on, suck me, my dear love, really suck me. From my own dry mouth I cannot suppress gasps of pleasure and disjointed words, 'Oh, darling, that's good, again, again.' And you tirelessly make me climax. My juices flow into your mouth and I beg for mercy.

Now we rest side by side. Your skin sticks to mine and I can feel my desire for you stirring again. No, my love, don't move. Stay there, my darling little god, your slave is going to adore you now. I bring my lips down onto your eyes, your gorgeous, adorable eyes alight with such intelligence, such energy, and such passion too, your glorious eyes which I love above all else. Then my mouth moves downwards and plants a long, ardent kiss on yours. My lips now travel over your chest, your stomach and your thighs, but when they reach that magnificent cock and those balls they end their descent. Ah, darling, give it to me, give me your beloved prick. I want to have all of him in my mouth. I suck him steadily and feel him gradually swell to this moist kiss. I cup your balls in my hands and the feel of it makes your entire body shudder.

With my hands I part the buttocks you have offered up to me, your perverse beloved. I know what you want. There, can you feel my tongue sliding inside you? It delves this intimate flesh which responds to its touch. I can feel you quivering with pleasure. My mouth sucks and licks, preparing the way for my arrogant cock.

Travelling down and up, up and down, its impressive head glides along the cleft of your arse. So that it can slide more easily into your tightly closed brown hole, I slip it into my wet cunt. Slick with my juices, how easily it probes into your arse which I do so adore! There, feel it, there. A little cry, 'oh, that's good', I know you can feel me in you. I'm taking you, my adorable mistress, I am your lover. And the miracle comes to pass, we change sexes. I pleasure myself over your buttocks and when I reach my climax my juices flow warm and soft over your skin. I scatter kisses over the brown hair at the back of your neck and drive my nails deep into you. But you have not had enough pleasure, my love. Come, kneel over my stomach. Tighten your fingers around your cock which has returned to its resting state. Make it swell, my loved one, just as I am making my button grow with my finger.

My lascivious eyes drink in this titillating tableau. Your hand goes up and down the length of your cock. Going quickly, quickly, then slowly to make the pleasure last. And I follow your every move. Let me see what you do when you are alone thinking of me. Remember Bandol, remember Narbonne where my extraordinary letters tormented you. Is this what you did? Tug, my love, tug on your darling prick.

But now your eyes suddenly light up. Your fingers tighten around your cock. It is stiff now, its head is swelling, a droplet appears, the first. Lean right over my body, darling Charles, look, I'm ready.

Ah, at last. Give it to me, give it. A jet of sperm springs forth, thick and white and still warm. It flows over my breasts, over my stomach. You have just spilled it irresistibly over your filthy mistress's body and she is moaning with pleasure at the feel of it.

Now I am more yours than ever. You have baptised me with your come. My whole body has felt its delicious warmth.

My darling love, I am perverted but I should like to be even more so to please you, to keep you, for I adore you, you know that. Your body gives me boundless intoxicating pleasure and in your arms I experience the most voluptuous ardour. If I too give this to you, my love, then I am happy, but my task is more arduous for I am not the only mistress of your senses and, alas, you can compare me to other caresses. So, you see, that is why I go to such lengths to find new refinements, ideas and attentions to try to fight, so that the time you spend in my arms is the best, so that this is what your senses prefer and long for, but, alas, shall I ever achieve that?

Think, my love, you think about it too, and tell me what you want. Am I truly the ardent mistress of your dreams? Or would you rather I were more gentle and passive?

One question has been burning my lips for a long time now, but would you answer should I ever ask it? And yet I would so like to know, oh yes, to know.

Goodbye, darling Lottie, I shall send you these long pages so that your thoughts are soon with me. Shall I see you this evening, my love?

A whole long week will go by when we shall not be free to love each other, but I do hope that we shall have the most ardent of sensations when next we can meet.

Ah, Charles, why does neither of us have a discreet, snug nest where we could be together? It would be so good to have our own 'home' where we could behave completely freely without worrying about neighbours. I have never missed the precious solitude I had in July as much as I do now. What wonderful times we would have in that room, my love!

Goodbye, you, I do love you. Passionate kisses to your darling lips and your glorious body, the body of a young god. Till this evening, perhaps, till tomorrow.

Your passionate mistress who adores you.

Simone

Oh, the appalling sadness that descended upon me, my dear love, when you were no more than a little black dot at the end of those endless platforms. With one last wave I bade you my farewell and when I realised I could no longer see you, I walked back the way we had come, side by side, just moments before.

Why did you leave me, darling Lottie, why did you leave me? Ten long days to live without you, far from you and your lips and your adorable eyes. I am appallingly sad, and for hours last night I kept seeing that relentless train, trundling, trundling, taking my love away. Oh, how I love you, my sweet darling, and how inescapably I am yours! Instead of diminishing my tenderness, every passing day reinforces it more surely, and I can no longer imagine my life without the warmth of your gaze, without the sweet brutality of your embraces, which have left their indelible imprint on every part of me, and which make my whole body quiver at the thought of them. I am passionately yours, I live for you, and for the hope of keeping you forever if you want that. I need to adore your glorious body, I need to swoon to the warm breath of your lips, and I need to feel your regal flesh taking furious possession of me, making me the happiest and most fulfilled of mistresses.

Oh, my darling love, keep me by your side, keep me in your arms. I love you, I love you to distraction.

My Charles, how did you spend last night? As I lay awake I could not stop thinking of the women who would be travelling through the night with you. I am so afraid of losing you, I am so afraid of everything, my loved one, that the least little thing alarms me and breaks my heart.

I am frantically looking forward to your long letter on Tuesday. I long for it with all my might. Will it be the letter my heart hopes it is? Will the distance between us kindle an ardent longing in you for all of my body, an ardent longing for my passionate and perverted attentions?

And yet how happy I was yesterday in the sadness of leaving you. I had you all to myself in that crowd of people, and you were kind, my little Lottie. I carry those memories in my heart, they will keep me company during your long absence.

I shall think about the profound happiness in store for us on your return. Ah, to be reunited with the intoxicating warmth of your body against mine, reunited with the glory of you.

I am nestling in your arms. Give me your lips, I want a long kiss from the bottom of our hearts. Remember all our couplings, darling Lottie, picture me in the most shocking of poses, unreservedly surrendering every part of my body, my cunt, my arse, my breasts, my mouth. Remember that all of it is yours, ready to give you the most ardent of climaxes, if that is your wish.

Do you want to keep me forever, my dear darling? Do you want to have me by your side, still loving and faithful? I would do anything not to leave you, to have you to myself forever. You are a wonderful lover, full of perversion, full of tenderness too, and spending an hour in your arms is all the happiness I need. I want to keep you forever, my sweet darling, and to take possession of your body for as long as you want me to. I shall never weary of your embraces or your kisses, never, ever.

I have managed to introduce you to this perverse, abnormal and salacious coupling, and if that is what your body wants and hopes to have, if you have not grown indifferent to this embrace, I myself love it and I shall treat you to it with undying ardour.

Whatever pleasures your desires dictate, you know I like them all. If you have new passions, tell me, I shall make them my own as I have already made your vices mine.

I love you so much, my sweet darling, that nothing about you could displease me. Are we not inexorably bound by our wonderful past? Remember all our lovemaking.

Oh, come back soon, darling Charles, come back soon. Remember I am waiting for you, all aquiver with love, waiting to throw myself into your arms and nestle against your heart.

How endless these ten days will feel! Write to me as often as you can, my dear love, I should be so sad with no news of you.

Remember that I am here waiting for you. I shall count the hours till I see you next.

Be good, my dear love, when you are far from me. I derive some relief from knowing you will be alone for a week. My sadness is somewhat alleviated, but I am afraid of that woman who was eyeing you yesterday evening. I hope she let you sleep in peace. And I also hope my letter kept you company all night and kept any temptation at arm's length.

No, come now, I'm teasing you, I trust you, my sweet darling. But I love you so passionately that I am afraid of losing you. You cannot resent me for that, surely.

I am not sure that I shall be able to write again before Monday. I was hoping to be alone for a week but at the last minute an unexpected complication has kept my family here, so I am not sure how I shall manage to write to you. If you receive no more letters before Tuesday, you will know that, despite my own wishes, I have had to forgo the pleasure of telling you everything my heart dictates to me.

Goodbye, my great love, I am putting my arms around your neck and pressing my lips to yours in a long, long kiss right from my heart which is so full of you.

Come back soon, do come back soon, I am waiting for you. Send me a long letter, a very tender, very passionate one. Tell me how much you think of me, and how you would like me to love you when next we meet. Goodbye, my sweet darling, I love you.

Your passionate mistress,

Simone

M y loved one,
    I had to wait until five o'clock yesterday before your longed-for letter arrived, and it felt as if the wretched day never wanted to end.

Imagine my impatience as I ripped open the two envelopes holding those passionate pages which I read with such profound joy. Yes, your letter is very much what I wanted, and I cannot stop rereading it.

So you do still think of me just as much as in the past, and the memory of my touch arouses you and maddens you when we are apart. I am so happy, my dear love. I was so afraid you had tired of my embraces and no longer loved me. Now I know, and it is an immeasurable pleasure thinking of the wonderful moments we shall spend together again.

You may be breathless with craving for my body, but, my loved one, you should know that when we are apart I am haunted relentlessly by your kisses. Like you, I want to press myself up against your body. I want to feel the extraordinary tingle of your skin against mine, and to make my own indelible imprint on you. I can think of nothing more wonderful, more blissful than the fusion of our two bodies. Before we engage in that ultimate furious embrace which leaves us exhausted, let us stay a while like this, lying against each other, close together, so close. Come to my arms, my loved one, I want to hold you to me, I want to breathe in the smell of your male flesh. I want to fondle every inch of your glorious nudity with my lips. Oh my beloved god, let me adore you, let me gaze on this wondrously beautiful body and hold it to my heart. We must not be too hasty today, we must savour that heavenly moment, the moment we are reunited, and then we can gradually feel desire accumulating inside us, desire for our more brutal and perverted embraces, for the abnormal couplings that our depravity has revealed to us.

My darling Lottie, I am picturing you in your room in Narbonne. You are lying naked on your bed rereading passionate letters from your mistress. Your beautiful body is calm and restful but slowly, gradually your hand ventures down between your splayed thighs. It reaches for and finds your twitching member and grasps it tightly between tense fingers. Your pink head swells with desire, your hand goes up, and down, goes up more quickly and tightens its grip, and you cannot tear your eyes away from the tantalising lines I wrote in one last desperate appeal to your flesh from mine. Think of my shameless buttocks, think of my tightening cunt and all the different ways I touch you, and then tug yourself, my loved one, tug yourself. I can just see the way your hand jerks, the way you close your eyes in ecstasy. Your lips open slightly to utter my name. And your huge prick bursting full of sperm. Tug yourself, darling Lottie, and when you come I shall be there to harvest the sap.

I want you passionately, my sweet darling, and I have a fierce longing to take you.

When you return I shall give you every inch of my body. And you will make me come with your ardent attentions. My loved one, I want to belong to you still more wildly. But is it possible to imagine more than we do together already? As I write to you now, I wish you were beside me. I wish I could feel your skin thrill to my touch, and feel your beautiful prick. I wish I could swallow it into my cunt, yes, I wish you would fuck me. I love you so much that I find myself wanting that most ordinary of couplings. Oh, how intoxicating to feel your stiffened member probing slowly inside my flesh. And I am no longer sure which I prefer.

Yes, Charles, we shall have some wild exploits on your return. Our bodies will be irresistibly joined together by our supernatural ramrods and we shall never be able to forget each other, no, never. You are my mistress, are you not? You are my lover, are you not? Do the two of us not comprise four bodies? Why would we look else-where for other pleasures which could never possibly match our mutual perversion? Couplings like ours are rare things. Don't you think? And what a miracle it is that we have managed to provide all these unsuspected ecstasies for each other! Would you ever dare ask another woman for such unusual and perverse attentions? Would you dare ask her to be your indefatigable male lover? And could you now give up such pleasures? And what about me? Do you believe I could ever experience such couplings in any other arms but yours? As you can see, my beloved Charles, we are inexorably bound to each other by our perversion and our love, and so long as we enjoy taking our pleasure in this way, we shall take our pleasure together.

I will have a new 'member' for your return. What madness! Tomorrow I shall tell you about the sadistic couplings we can have together. I hope to have another letter from you this evening, I shall reply to it and you will find my reply when you arrive on Monday.

Goodbye, my dear love, four more days to get through without you. But then I shall have you. I shall have you and I shall give myself to you with every ounce of my being, with all my heart.

My lips on yours in a swooning kiss.

Simone

My dear love,

I have just received your letter from Clermont. How entrancing of you to have written so often, and I shall reward you on your return. I am now counting the hours. Each one brings you a little closer to me. Each one shaves another parcel of time off our separation, and in only a few days I shall be with you again at last. This long week spent far from your embrace has been a sad time, but that is as I would want it, because our future happiness depends upon it. Had we both had only vague feelings of regret to be parting, it would have been the end. But how much more ecstatically our love will blossom again now! How much sweeter our every caress will feel after this separation which weighs so heavily on our hearts as well as our senses!

Ah, my darling little Lottie, I too need your glorious body. I need to have you in my arms, quivering with vices and desires, and I cannot wait for the wonderful moment when my lips can at last reclaim every inch of you. How I shall love you, oh, how I shall love you! Yes, you are as truly filthy a mistress as I am, and I will ably rekindle the wildest of longings in you. You will find me more passionate than ever, for this long absence has exacerbated my desire for your body.

117

I close my eyes and picture you lying on the bed. There in the half-light, all your beauty lies before me. And I kneel fervently before you, trailing my burning lips over your tingling body. You are beautiful, my dear lover, and I adore you. Let me savour the smell of your skin, let me prostrate myself on this nakedness which is mine alone for the space of an hour. At last I shall hold you in my arms without any constraints, and I shall make your whole being reach a devastating climax.

I know which ardent ministrations you expect of me. Every ounce of you longs for the unforgettable sensations that my vice alone can afford you. And you want my lips, my tongue and finger to delve shamelessly into your little brown hole. You want to drive your hard prick deep into my throat or squeeze it between my breasts. My whole body is yours. Every part of it belongs to you, and I shall do everything I can to arouse you passionately until you spill the come wherever you choose.

But there are four of us now. We shall commit every folly and we shall stop only when we are quite spent and powerless.

And I want to give you a new form of passion. I now want you to experience the bite of the whip, I want it to leave its searing mark on your skin as it has on mine. Come on, lie down, bury your head in the pillow. I settle on your rump, my powerful thighs imprisoning your buttocks. There you are, look, now it is your turn to suffer, just as you made me suffer. The leather lashes flail your skin relentlessly and your swollen prick pulses a little harder with every blow.

But you beg for mercy. Come and give me your magnificent arse so I can kiss it and you can forget the torture. Oh, how I love this delicious little hole which is just asking to be kissed! My tongue probes irresistibly inside you, and prepares the way for the formidable member clasped in my hand. Yes, darling Lottie, yes, I am going to bugger you, for I understand your crowning passion. This is the wonderful ministration you want. There, there. Oh, I am so deep inside you, my love! Can you feel my colossal prick deep in your arse? Give me your cock, I'm going to suck it. Give me your balls, I want to lick them, and you must take my cunt between your lips and suck me, suck me.[13]

---

13 Simone is becoming increasingly dominating and wants to take revenge on Charles and make him suffer – however, this is only in her imagination, and the reality is that she offers Charles the choice of whether he wants to experience this pain. She comments later in the letter that she will 'meekly comply' with his decision. This indicates that while they may have playfully swapped gender roles, and Simone is making suggestions, it is obviously Charles who makes the decisions. She gives us the impression that she is the one proposing every single new fantasy, but in fact she is just trying to guess what would please her lover, and when she realises, as seems to be the case in this letter, that he has no masochistic propensity, she promptly drops her suggestion and abandons herself to his desires. Although this does not prevent her from continuing to inspire her lover with wild scenarios.

Please be here soon, be here soon. I cannot wait to climax in your arms. I cannot wait to savour this new intoxicating delight. It must feel so good! How happy we shall be to see each other again, my dear love! It is so long since our bodies melded together, and my desire is surging up inside me, tireless and all-powerful. My little god, I am happy I have revealed my longing for this sadistic act. And I do so hope you will never tire of it so that you keep me in your arms forever. I shall be your lover for as long as you would like, my loved one.

I shall go to pick up the new 'member' tomorrow, but alas, I fear it will be another week before we can try it out, for I shall have much to do this week, and I cannot be sure I can be free for an hour before the end of the week. Our next rendezvous will most likely be on Saturday. But we shall be reunited this Monday. Well, we can discuss the possibility of being alone together soon for, just like you, I am impatient to be with you so we can commit all the follies our vices have invented.

And do tell me by letter whether you are prepared to experience the ordeal of the whip. Tell me whether you are ready to suffer as I have suffered for you.

As I have said, the sensation is certainly unforgettable. It is impossible to distinguish the pain from the pleasure, and this combination of cruelty and happiness is astonishing and intoxicating. But, darling, it truly is an ordeal. Just remember how my body quailed to your blows! Think on it, I shall comply meekly with your wishes.

120

You may still dream of making me suffer, it may please you to bruise my flesh, but at least I know that when I take you from behind I give you an ardent climax you had long dreamed of experiencing but did not dare request. Your vice serves you well, my dear love, and you have at last been able to give it free rein. You wanted a male member in your arse, delving your flesh in every direction. You wanted to experience this ultimate intoxication and I gave it to you. Like you, my dear love, I feel that 'nothing can equal this perverse coupling'. What more delicious pleasure than feeling one's flesh being so furiously violated, and feeling faint with delight in a lover's arms!

Oh, how desperately I long to be in your arms again, to be quite naked and to offer you my arse, my cunt and my lips, and to take you with a great irresistible thrust of my ramrod into the innermost depths of your being. Think it over, tell me whether you want to savour the cruel spanking I have in store for you at our next assignation, or whether you should like to wait longer. I shall want you so very much, my loved one, that I fear I shall not have the heart to make you suffer. My longing for your flesh is a longing for tenderness and passion, but I shall do your bidding. Command and I shall blindly obey. And yet the thought of it is profoundly arousing. To give you pleasure through pain, how delicious! Oh, come back quickly, darling Lottie, quickly. I cannot wait to hold you to my beating heart, to feel your soft skin again, to have your mouth, your eyes, your hair, your hands, oh, all of you.

I am waiting for your last letter with terrible impatience. Will it arrive tomorrow? I shall put my three replies into the same envelope and you will find them on your return. Will they satisfy you?

Goodbye, my dear love. Only three more days tomorrow evening. I am haunted by a demented impatience for your every attention. How we shall love each other, my Charles! Make sure your pretty little arse is good and ready. It will suffer brutal assaults after this long absence. How happy I shall be to probe your flesh. I feel I can see you already and my ramrod is hard for you, furiously hard. There, look, I have you now, I am taking you, buggering you, oh, I'm buggering you, my adorable darling, and I'm coming between your buttocks. Ah, it feels too good! Come back quickly.

Simone

M y darling doll,

Tell me why I feel sad this morning. My heart is weighed down by boundless sorrow and I have come to pour my feelings into yours to dispel this burden. I shall see you later, my sweet darling, you will keep me close to you. You will let your tender gaze linger on my eyes, and your beloved mouth will halt the bitter words on my lips.

If you only knew how blissful it is taking refuge in your arms. If you only knew how precious it is having your longed-for self beside me. For nearly a year now, thanks to you, I have experienced profound happiness, ardent embraces and sometimes even sweet tenderness. How I love you, my darling Charles, when you wrap me in all your kindness, when you are more loving and gentle. If you only knew how I long for the way you sometimes gaze at me with a happy lover's eye. Apart from you, I have nothing, nothing in life that appeals to me.

Forgive me, my little one, for giving free rein to my sadness but, you see, there are times in life when the heart feels too full, too heavy, and it breaks. Welcome me into your arms, my dear darling, open them wide to me and wrap them around my poor body, lull my unhappiness to sleep. You alone can cure it.[14]

I need all your love, my Lottie, you know that. Look, it is not long now until we reach a whole year. The thought that I have managed to keep you so long makes me very happy. You could have slipped away from me after our first embrace. I too could have tired of loving you. But not at all. We are still passionate lovers, and we fully savour the joys of our frenetic couplings.

Soon we shall spend another wonderful hour together, just like the last. Goodness, what fire we put into loving each other, did we not, my Lottie? Oh, your body, your adorable body, I do so love it! Oh, the passion with which I still clasp it to me and the joy I experience when I truly possess your innermost flesh! You give yourself to me with no reservations or shame. You long for my most outrageous ministrations, and you savour them with the same ardour I feel for yours to me. We have the same sensations. There is nothing we have not discovered now

---

14 We are now aware that Simone experiences frequent ups and downs. The lovers have big arguments, before passionate reconciliations, and Simone frequently falls into depression without being able to say why. She would have made an ideal patient for Dr Freud, but she does not seem to have any interest in self-analysis, or even to be conscious of her problems, despite her neurosis becoming obvious to the reader. We do not know whether she was aware of Sigmund Freud, but it is doubtful. His work was beginning to appear in translation at this time, but few people in France were interested in psycho-analysis.

and, if this is what you want, we shall continue to have such unforgettable moments for which we both still long. Keep me as your mistress, keep me as your lover for as long as you like. All of me is yours, with no need to share me and no restrictions. I am yours in my heart and my flesh, and my whole body belongs to you. I want your extravagant caresses and your arousing kisses, I want you to take me. And give me your body too. I adore it and I have not yet conquered it completely. I want to cover your body with my own excited body. I want to force my perverse couplings onto you as you force your vices onto me. I am a prisoner to your desires, but I want you in turn to be a slave. I pin you down with my arms, between my thighs, and you cannot resist my demented exploits which make you die of pleasure. I penetrate you gently but irrefutably, and you can feel me deep inside you, my ramrod that never falters and never tires. Oh, the madness of that moment when you finally belong to me! Nothing could tear you from my arms and I collapse onto your shuddering body, kissing it passionately. I love you, I love you, darling Lottie. Till later. I cannot wait to be tightly in your arms. I want to feel your mouth on mine. And until I can feel your beloved prick straining frantically in my hand, I suck on you wildly, darling love. Go on, let it go, I shall swallow it all.

Your Simone

Thursday, nine in the evening

My dear darling,

Everyone has left. I am alone, all alone in this vast, silent house until midnight. The street is dark, with just a small light over there breaking through the darkness. A small light I know so well, one that makes my heart leap in my breast. It is perched right up on high and I cannot take my eyes off it. You cannot imagine the full extent of the joy – and the sadness too – to be had from staring at that little light. Joy, yes of course, because of this thought: 'He is there, beneath that light, there so close by. If I cried his name wildly into the steady darkness, he would hear me.' But an appalling, cruel sadness immediately constricts my heart: 'Yes, he is there but he is not alone. What words are being said to him right now? How does he look at the woman saying them? And later, later when this little light goes out, what will he do with her?'

Oh, Charles, my one and only, my great love, can you ever know how obsessed I am by such thoughts? Can you ever know what torments I endure and how much I suffer because of Her?! Oh, please don't get that harsh look in your eye, understand me. You know how much

I love you, you know the ardent caresses I want to bestow on your whole body. So you must realise that every inch of me rebels and suffers at the very thought of your adored body quivering with pleasure to another woman's kisses. It is such a horrible image and it haunts me, it haunts me, it hurts me!

I can do nothing about it and never shall. I must love you with this other woman permanently between us, but I am very sad this evening, Charles. Forgive me for talking to you like this, but I need to describe my pain because it weighs heavily on me, very heavily. I love you, I love you with an unbounded love, you know that, and, alas, there is no love without suffering.

But, my dear darling, these are not the words you wanted to hear. You like me better when I am not so lyrical and affectionate. And yet that is very much a cry from the heart that I have just given you.[15]

---

15 Had she been analysed at the time, Simone may well have been diagnosed with 'hysteria'. This would explain why she goes through peaks and troughs of enthusiasm and depression when she realises that her desires do not match her lover's. She therefore embodies a form of hysterical neurosis, which has led her to become the other, to the point of borrowing Charles's gender. While clearly distressing for Simone, without this particular psychic disorder her correspondence might have been much less interesting. Although this element of her personality made her a remarkable and unusual lover, we can understand why it might have been a burden, in the long run, for Charles.

Will it be tomorrow, my love? I hope so with all my might. Tomorrow, if this is what you want, I shall hold you in my arms, all of you, and I shall treat you to my softest, sweetest caresses, and my most sadistic too, all the ministrations you love, all those you want.

Dear darling, quickly throw off all the clothes hiding your glorious body. Look, I am already naked and waiting impatiently for you. While you undress, I perform for you the lascivious acts that I resort to when I am far from your eyes, plying my cunt with a headstrong finger and fondling my arse. Watch, my love, watch. My cunt is yearning for the sublime attentions of your tongue. Oh, come and bury your mouth between my lips. Come and gather the abundant flow of juices. Can you feel it wetting your throat? Suck, my dear love, suck me hard. It is such a blissful feeling. Take my button, take it, bring me to a devastating climax. I want to be left powerless in your arms.

Oh, the adorable hole and your beautiful buttocks, it is such a pleasure touching it with my inflamed lips, my tongue, my fingers . . . I love feeling this warm soft flesh deep inside you, and its strange thrilling sensations. The pleasure makes it tighten around my finger. And later it will be my turn to take you. I want to pleasure you slowly with expert restraint. I want the climax to build inside you gradually. Give me your beautiful arse, darling love. Sit yourself astride my ramrod so that it reaches deep inside you. There, right there, slowly, darling, slowly. Can you feel me penetrating inexorably deeper inside you? Is it good, tell me, is it good? I'm buggering you, I'm buggering you, I'm inside you. Lie down on me, my love, feel the magnificent ramrod being pulled from your hole and making you come. Drive your swollen prick into my cunt or into my arse, whichever you like. I want us to climax together. I want to see our two bodies on top of each other. I want to feel our flesh melting together, our most intimate parts indistinguishable from each other. I want to feel my cunt between your lips, and your cock in my cunt, in my arse, everywhere, everywhere.

My dear loved one, be free tomorrow. I want you so much. I need to feel you owning me entirely, irresistibly.

Yes, my love, I know you like this perverse abnormal coupling, so I shall always let you have it, for there is nothing I like more than buggering you. I like creating the strange illusion that I am not a woman but the handsome lover your perversity hopes to meet. When you feel me on your back, when I imprison you between my powerful thighs, forget that I am a woman. It is your lover's prick probing you. There, can you feel it? Look how big and hard it is, and look how well it knows the way into your hole. Tomorrow you can enjoy this perverse sensation once more. Tomorrow I shall bugger you passionately because I adore you. Goodbye, my little Lottie, I shall go to bed now thinking of you, but I shall behave. I want to keep all my strength for tomorrow. I want it to be your attentions and your impassioned kisses that make me come. I want to feel your swollen prick deep inside. You will put him in just a little to kindle my pleasure, just the head. I shall drench him with my come and you will spray yours in the depths of my cunt. I want you to bugger me, for that is the ultimate coupling, the one that leaves us powerless. Till tomorrow, my dear love. Telephone soon with the good news. I shall be as filthy as you like.

My lips on yours, tomorrow.

Your Simone

The 'other woman', Charles's wife, is an invisible but constant protagonist in this story, and the jealousy she inspires – jealousy that tortures Simone – emerges as one of the motives for the extraordinary passion. In an earlier letter Simone fretted about the women who would be travelling in the same compartment as her lover. Later on, she was still worrying: 'Would you ever dare ask another woman for such unusual and perverse attentions?'

And now, alone in her room, she gives vent to her powerless despair as she pictures him, so close to her own home, sharing his life and his bed with his legitimate wife.

Without this element of jealousy, Simone might not have been so inventive, and might not have driven the sexuality of her relationship with Charles to extremes that she knew he could never reach with his wife. Now the preserve of his lover, sodomy became a token of exclusivity.

M y dear loved one,
      Yes, I received your letter, and it was just as I
had hoped. You are very obedient, very tender and very
sweet, and I adore you. I am writing to you from my
quiet, lonely little bedroom. It is pelting with rain outside,
and the garden is steeped in darkness. I am snug in here
thinking of you, of us, perfectly at my leisure to reread
the delicious words in your last letter. All the words I
longed to hear are music to my ears, and they reverberate
all around my heart, mingling with the echo of your
darling name which I so often whisper to myself.

Just a week, my dear darling, just a few more days to
get through and I shall be in your arms to celebrate our
first anniversary. I cannot think of it without a tremendous feeling of joy, nor without feeling considerably
aroused, for I remember all the tenderness we have
exchanged and all the blissful caresses we have experienced throughout that year.

My darling, you asked me what it feels like for me when
I pin you in my arms and drive my deft member deep,
deep inside you. It is a peculiar sensation. I feel I am no
longer myself. When I touch you I become a man and it

132

is with a man's desire that I take you and fuck you. A violent demented passion inflames my blood and I take pleasure in your body as you do in mine. Yes, I shall always want to give you this ultimate coupling for that is how I achieve true pleasure. Seeing your body offering itself, seeking mine, feeling your flesh giving way to my practised pressure and taking you furiously. Oh, the intoxication of it, what an unforgettable and endlessly desirable moment! And, if you want to, you shall be my mistress again on Friday. In our new nest, you will discover the full ardour of my desire, and you will be mine, with no constraints and no need to share. We shall belong entirely and most wildly to each other, and we shall climax together.

We can savour all our most daring ministrations, for there will be nothing to stand in the way of our depravity. We shall outstrip each other and rival each other in our ardour. How happy we shall be!

It is a long time now since any qualms have held us back, and our love is all the more exalted for it, all the more beautiful. If we did not love each other as we do, do you think that we could look at each other without disgust afterwards, as we go about our daily lives? No, Charles, no, my darling. But we do love each other, nothing we do is dirty, and everything we do is necessary to our love. I feel that very strongly. I am proud now that I am quite sure you find me attractive, you love my body and it makes yours happy. Oh, tell me you are happy. Do with me whatever you want, I am yours.

Sometimes when I leave your arms, replete with you but still wanting you, I think about this and realise it would be impossible for us not to exploit our bodies together the way we do, for our hearts and senses are so attuned we could not possibly stop loving each other. With everything that we have done together, we simply could not part now, and the chains we have created for ourselves will never weigh on us.

This evening I am casting my mind back over the wonderful times when we have taken each other with great fury or great tenderness. I am also thinking of all the joys I did not know until you made me your mistress, your instrument of joy. After what we have done together, it would be impossible for me to look for another lover because you know what it is, you know what we do, Charles. We melt together, we bind our bodies together, we are reduced to just one flesh, we become just one creature, and when our embrace slackens and you withdraw from me, I am acutely aware of being a part of you and you a part of me. My body has absorbed something of yours and given you the best of itself.

I owe you a boundless happiness, the happiness of belonging to you, to you who made me as I am now. And I am yours, nothing but yours, forever, I know that, and I am happy in this state of slavery, and I want to thank you, my handsome lover, my love.

No, I cannot believe we shall ever separate. We have been too happy together, and should it ever happen, what a disaster it would be! But no, the joys we have savoured, the magnificent ecstasies which have made you cry out involuntarily, which have seen me sprawl onto you panting and utterly spent, which have made us sleep the sleep of the dead, which have afforded us hours of delight, all that will continue. What we have done and what we still want to do will keep our happiness intact and you will *never* be able to give yourself to another woman without thinking of when you gave yourself to me.

Now, you know how I should like you to give yourself to me. I want you to submit to all my most outlandish attentions, my most daring embraces, for on that date which is blessed among dates, I want you to be completely enslaved to my body. You will leave my body only when your limbs ache, when you are exhausted with pleasure and voluptuous delights, when you are brimful with vice and passion. I adore you and I need to take you and to give myself to you at the same time. Only one more week, and you will have me naked in your arms. You will be free to caress every inch of this body which is thrilling in anticipation of the pleasure. You will be able to hold it between your thighs, to beat it or to kiss it. But remember that it will take its revenge and it will offer you the most sublime coupling. Your whole body shivers at the memory of it. You can look forward to that moment with great confidence. You shall have the wildest of climaxes, my most darling darling.

Goodbye, till Monday. I am thinking of you so much. In my thoughts I already have your delicious body to myself. Take me too, I surrender myself to you because I love you passionately. I shall see you soon.

My mouth on yours in an intoxicating kiss.

I cannot write any more. My *pneu* would be too heavy and I am afraid I shan't have time to bring it to your office. I love you.

Simone

Saturday, eleven o'clock

My dear darling love,
   I should have liked to have a long letter from you to which I could reply this evening. I shall have to call on my memories once more to fill these blank pages.

Did I fully express the extent of my joy when I left your arms yesterday? I doubt it, for your ardent attentions left me in such a state, I must have forgotten a good many things.

I cannot think of that divine hour without tingling from head to toe. How dreamy it was! What an exquisite experience I had and how you steered me to those volup- tuous delights! I had so hoped that we should be even happier than usual that day but, my dear love, I never thought we could reach such wonderful heights.

Remember it, Lottie, remember.

We met in our delightful new nest, in the welcoming calm of that big bedroom.[16] I was barely in your arms

---

16 This 'nest' was probably a rented room in a discreet apartment building. Renting a room like this would have been very unusual practice for a young lady at the time when it would have been a man's role to take such an initiative. This is another example of how Simone behaves as though she is a man with

before I felt you already impressively erect. You were on the bed before I was, but I soon come to join you, aquiver with ardent longing. The very touch of your soft white skin makes me thrill and I press myself to you, holding your whole body tightly to me. Your cock is hard and so big. I offer him my cunt as a haven, and he plies right into me without a moment's hesitation. It feels so good! We stay like that for a while, not moving. I come slowly to the strokes of your warm soft prick. Charles darling! You were a wonderful lover.

But now it is my turn to give you the promised release. Give me your arse, right here, my dear love. I do long for it so. I find the beloved little brown hole, latch onto it with my avid mouth. I suck it and bite it and kiss it ardently. I hold all of it between my lips, and you groan with pleasure. Your sighs fan the flames of my ardour. Instead of stopping, I continue more forcefully. You drive your nails into my wrists, abandoning yourself to me helplessly. You are already delirious at this stage, but I want even more. To take ultimate possession of your flesh, that is what I want so ardently, and the time is coming. Lovingly and well aware of the ecstasy I have in store for you, I prepare my 'member' for battle. You gasp with pleasure, you can feel your climax building. My breasts are like two big balls knocking against your buttocks. Tell me, my love, is it good? But you beg for mercy. I withdraw

a mistress; Simone was surely atypical in her capacity to reverse roles and become the other.

my member and press myself up to you. My engorged button strokes your quivering hole and I climax wildly between your buttocks.

But your desire has not been assuaged. What you want, I know, is to make me suffer cruelly. You grab one of my ankles and bring your arm crashing down; it is such a brutal blow that I cry out in pain. But, impervious to my pleas, you keep me at your mercy and spank my rump from left to right and right to left, harder and harder. I cannot take any more. One last blow. You finally take pity on me and, to help me forget, you press your mouth to my cunt once more, and my pain evaporates as I come.

So, darling, it was time for the final coupling. We could resist our desire no longer. You managed to hold yourself off long enough for me to feel you inside me and it was exquisite, my adorable lover. I felt everything, everything, right to the last drop of sperm, and I gave myself to you passionately.

My darling, it is a long time since we have experienced such joy. That hour will feature as one of our most sublime among all those we have spent together.

We celebrated our first anniversary with insatiable eagerness. We were wonderful lovers, would you not agree?

I should like to know what you thought, darling Lottie. I feel I succeeded in making you happy too, and in sating all your desires, but I should like you to confirm that in words.

I did everything I could to avoid disappointing you. I had promised so much. Did I manage to keep my promises? I left your arms quite spent. Your passionate attentions exhausted me and I was still very tired this morning. But, oh, the memories I shall have of you, my wonderful lover! Oh, the skill with which you handle my body!

Darling, I do so wish you could have that wonderful sensation at last, the one you admitted to me in your passion. My hand struck your proffered rump twice but you denied yourself further beating, even though the place was perfectly suitable for that particular ordeal.

Do you not want to experience that ultimate caress, then? I myself cannot wait to inflict it on you, for I know the profound joy it would bring you. Now that we have found our charming haven, you are at your leisure to acclimatise me to your ever more cruel spankings. I shall not refuse to suffer if it means you will love me more.

For a year now I have succumbed to your every desire. I have anticipated your least little whim. I have invented perverse ministrations for you and, thanks to all this, I can still have every inch of you.

I cannot cope without you now, it would be impossible. I am appallingly sad when I do not have you with me. I watched you sleeping yesterday. You lay with your head between your arms, calm after such energetic antics. Your naked body displayed all its charm for me to see. Do you know you are beautiful, my dear love, and that I am very proud to have a lover such as you? Just at the thought of that, I can feel my desire for you. I should like to have you by my side this evening, darling Lottie. I should like to be free to kiss your skin passionately once more, and drive my tongue between your buttocks. I adore that arse, it belongs to me. I want it all to myself. The moment I am deprived of it, there is only one thing I want: to have it back. Oh, why are you not completely mine? Why do I have to share you with another woman who has no idea of all the pleasures she is neglecting to give you? Ah, there, look, it is starting again. When I was in our nest I felt calm, but I am going out of my mind again this evening. I love you too much to tolerate sharing you, and if I knew that you were as happy in her arms as you are in mine, it would be over, you know. In order to have any peace, I need to be under the illusion that I am the beloved mistress whose every caress you desire. If that were not the case, if you felt the same joy with Her as you do with me, I would give up the fight, I swear it.

Darling Charles, I have suddenly become spiteful this evening. I am jealous, horribly jealous, and my whole body flinches at the thought that, at this very moment, as I write, you are asleep beside another woman. I shall sleep all alone, thinking of you. Why can I not fall asleep after a wonderful lovemaking like yesterday's? What a wonderful mistress you are, Lottie, and how could I cope without you? If you want me as your lover, keep me as long as you like. I hope the day never comes when we part, and that we are now setting out towards our next anniversary.

I shall stop, darling treasure, it is past midnight. I shall send this letter as a *pneu* first thing on Monday. You probably will not have time to reply, but I should love to read your words after our special day. Beloved Lottie, tell me soon whether you are pleased with your lover. And also tell me you love me. I need to hear that again.

Goodbye, darling love, I am ardently kissing your mouth which is so good at sucking my cunt, and I am buggering you wildly, for as long as you can bear it. I shall send myself to sleep by pleasuring my button and imagining it is your hand making me come.

I adore you.

Your Simone

My dear little god,

I feel infinitely sad today. My heart is weighed down by an obscure, indefinable sadness, and it hurts. Jumbled thoughts haven been spinning around inside my head, and I do wish I had you beside me, close beside me, to comfort me with your beloved presence, to feel the gentle pressure of your arm against mine as I did yesterday. A little later I shall telephone you just to hear your voice.

If we could meet up in our little room today, how I would love you, my darling one. What passionate fervour I would put into kissing those warm lips which surrender to my kisses. I would treat them to a long caressing kiss, full of ardour but also tenderness, an endless kiss to express all the violence of my towering love for you. Next, picture it, I shall draw your beloved brown-curled head to me with both my hands, and then your huge eyes would be within reach of my lips, your deep, passionate eyes which have me under their spell, and whose gaze is sometimes clouded by the full force of your desire. And I shall close your beloved eyes with my lips while I softly, gently stroke the pearly skin all over your glorious body which affords me such incomparable ecstasies, all your male flesh to which my whole being cleaves with a confounding desire, robbing me of my strength and my will. If I had you in my arms, my dear love, I should like to intoxicate you with my wild caresses before carrying you off to the infinite ecstasies into which both our bodies sink.

Will this happen tomorrow? I desperately hope so, my dear love, for it feels a long time since you pleasured my body with your ardent kisses.

Will it be tomorrow that you hold me in your fervent arms once more? Do tell me. Oh, I hope so, I hope so, for I do long for you terribly!

My body still faithfully carries within it the magical memory of our last tryst. Remember our two naked bodies intertwined, your hot avid mouth pressed to my hardened button. Your wonderfully skilled tongue licks all this eager intimate flesh which gradually releases its bitter sap into your mouth. I take your cock into my impatient mouth and feel it stiffen, then, abandoning this pulsing member, I stroke your tempting brown balls. I take one between my lips, into my mouth, and now it has completely dis-appeared. Even ten days later I still think I can feel it deep inside my throat, and it is as if I am swooning with pleasure all over again to the insistent caress of your tongue.

Are these the follies we shall commit tomorrow? Which coupling shall we favour? I shall do everything you want, my love. I shall lie passively beside you, and you can direct our senses in whichever direction pleases you.

Tell me, do you want to make me suffer? Are you obsessed with that fiercest of pleasures? Do you want to make me shriek with pain under your blows? How arousing you find it watching your mistress's poor body contorting before you! How your cock responds to her screams, and what ecstasy when her battered rump produces that first drop of blood which your cruel depravity has waited so long to see!

I am prepared to suffer anything, to accept anything if I know you are happy, if I know that you love me, for I want to keep you a long time, a very long time, my dear little god, my adorable lover.

I know that if you want to, you will make me suffer terribly, but also what joy I shall have in my reward! You will take me in such a soft, tender embrace that I shall forget the excruciating flagellation. My whole body belongs to you, you know that. You are my only master, master of my heart and master of my senses. So, you decide. Tell me the best position. On my knees, I can present you with my shameless rump. Is that how you want me? No, like this instead: flat on my stomach with my hands bound and my legs spread but also tied down, and with a cushion under my stomach to raise my impertinent arse towards you. Look, it's taunting you, making fun of you. Make it stop with a fearsome beating to lacerate it until it bleeds.

Oh, Charles, darling Charles, to suffer like that for you, what ecstasy! I shall bring a magnificent strap tomorrow if you want. What a terrifying toy in your expert hands! You must tell me if you want that or if you would rather be gentle and tender. I shall do whatever you want, but please don't make me wait any longer for this wonderful tryst. Come to my arms tomorrow, they are wide open, waiting to close around you with such passion.

But tell me you love me, tell me you want me. Don't have that hard, impenetrable expression which chills my heart. I know you are not free as you would wish, but do tell me once and for all that you love me, say it clearly and from this admission I shall draw the strength to bear your transient frostiness. Tell me I should not be alarmed when you are in that mood and indifferent to me, tell me you will gradually come back to me.

Yes, I know we have a wonderful past and an even more passionate present, but you know I fear the future. Alas, I do! And when I see you with that hard expression I feel horribly afraid our future will be here very soon. My little god, if you were not a remarkable lover, if you had not pleasured me in such unique ways, would I be so afraid of losing you? Surely I would believe others after you could make love to me, should I want them to? But you, you are not like the others. Do these 'others' know such ministrations, such orgies? And could I experience a love like this anywhere but in your arms? No, my Charles. Besides you, nothing matters. My flesh is irrevocably bound to yours, and that is why I am afraid of losing you.

But, reassure me, my darling treasure. Make me die with your kisses. Make me suffer with your passion. Take all of me, wildly, helplessly, I belong to you.

Listen, if you ever weary of my attentions, we shall part, but promise me you will tell me so frankly. I shall be strong and I shall listen. Rather a sad reality than appalling doubts gnawing at me . . .

Enough of such sad thoughts. I shall dream of you all night, my Loved One. You will fill my dreams with passionate images. Remember I am waiting for our next assignation with furious impatience. Don't make me wait any longer. Tomorrow if you can, perhaps the day after tomorrow, but as soon as possible, my beloved.

I am picturing all the wonder of your glorious body, and I can feel a wave of urgent longing rising within me. Belonging to you in pain or in pleasure, what unbounded delight!

Goodbye, my dear adorable little god. I shall expect a telephone call from you tomorrow, and I do hope it won't be a disappointment. If, like me, you cannot wait to relive the follies we have shared, you will do anything to come and join me. I am prepared to suffer. I promise to be compliant. Promise me you will love me with the full force of your depravity.

Goodbye, my dear love. I shall go home very soon so that I can entertain wild thoughts of you, of us.

Passionate kisses on your lips and your eyes. I am utterly yours.

Simone

My most adored darling,

    True to my promise, I am wasting no time in replying to the delicious long letter I found in the office this morning. It was certainly worth the wait, for every sentence was at once passionate and tender. Those are the bewitching words I love reading, for they make me happy.

If you only knew, my pretty darling, how good it feels to know you love me that much. I often have to convince myself it is true because this is all so magical that I keep thinking a dream so sweet must surely come to an end. But you mean it sincerely, I can tell, and look how radiant that makes me.

Yes, you will definitely succeed in binding me to you for another year, another whole year, because, my lover, your caresses are the kind to enthral, to enslave, and there is no power great enough to erase the memory of them, unless we choose to end them. But we must not restrict our mutual desire to this new year, for why would we weary of each other, my darling? Does our love not afford us the truest, deepest, greatest joys, and sensations so wonderful they do not seem real? We have long since stripped each other of all modesty or selfishness, and before seeking our own gratification, we each strive for the other's pleasure, wanting to make it complete and absolute. You know my vices and I know yours. They are similar, they are almost the same, and the perfect union of our bodies, as we battle out these vices, gives us undying memories for the rest of our lives.

Yes, darling Lottie, for some time I had been hoping to break away from bland, ritual couplings that leave me quite indifferent with no sense of desire, in the hopes of tasting new, almost unsuspected perverse pleasures. To achieve this, I dreamed of an adorable mistress who would give me her entrancing and depraved body, who would smother me with such sweet caresses that I would be left powerless . . . I searched for a long time but never found my Chosen Girl. And also, I hope you understand, I always hesitated at the last moment; I was not bold enough, and dared not confront this danger and put myself beyond the bounds of what is 'natural'. When fate in all its omnipotence brought us together, when I saw the ardent glow in your eyes as they stared at me, it was like a physical impact, a shock. I was deeply disturbed, without understanding why . . . I remained in that state for several days, unable to drive away the image glimpsed all too quickly. I thought of you obstinately, unrelentingly, and your eyes, your wonderful eyes that I do so adore, they were what I wanted to see again, to find again. Now that I know who we are, now that I can think over what we do, I realise that this shock was a secret signal: I had finally found the adorable creature I had searched for in

149

vain. I put up very little resistance to your advances, would you not say? I very soon made you my lover, before I truly knew you. And, do you know, I was often ashamed of that? Did you ever misjudge me? Do tell me. You can tell me now, now that we know each other. Here, this evening, I am revealing all my remorse, and there was plenty, but how short-lived it was! Under the effects of your tender passion, it melted like snow in sunlight, and now I have no regrets, none at all.

Yes, my love, in you I have found the most enticing mistress anyone could dream of finding. I wanted a charming body: do you not lay before me all the splendours of your flesh which is so soft, so white and so pure? Its every line is full and harmonious, delicious little breasts, a soft, polished stomach, a rounded rump, just fat enough to create the charming illusion for me. I wanted vice, and surely I have found it in you? And how ardently you long for my touch, how fierily eager you are to reciprocate it!

Oh, Lottie, my charming little mistress, you are the Chosen Girl, the one I was hoping to find. When I hold your body in my arms and kiss your skin, I am endlessly happy, for I adore you.

But as well as the unexpected role you have played to such perfection, what a wonderful lover I found in you! Passionate, perverse, sometimes brutal, occasionally tenderly loving. You are all these things, and you handle my body like a true virtuoso. You have managed to find forgotten regions to make every inch of me thrill. In your arms, I truly am a pitiful thing, almost a lifeless doll because you take my life, you draw it out of my body, you rob me of it drop by drop with your knowing kisses and your wonderful embraces. From the first day, you showed me the most adorable caresses, which made me yours till the end of days. Darling Charles, you have given me the most perfect, flawless happiness for a year now. Thanks to you, I know all the sweetness of love, I know its every desire, its every secret. My most fervent wish is to keep your tenderness for a long time, forever, because I adore you, I really do . . . What is any other man compared to you? Nothing, nothing . . . All I see in life is the gleam in your eyes, the red of your lips and the whiteness of your skin, and my horizon is wherever your heart stops.

Yes, my darling love, in a few more weeks you will be mine without any need to share. You will be a passionate lover to me alone, and I shall at last experience the ultimate ordeal you crave. You will feel the pain of the lash on your already smarting skin, you will have that double sensation, and you can finally tell me whether I have succeeded in initiating you to the cruel mysteries of flagellation. Oh, quickly, Charles, roll on the day when I am master of your body at last, and you give yourself to me unreservedly.

In our perfectly discreet room, we can share the most ardent joys. We shall most likely be together again soon, quite helplessly and completely together.

You know I can no longer survive without your body. I need you more than ever now, your lips, your hands, your eyes, oh, especially your eyes full of longing. Give it all to me, my love!

I give myself to you entirely. You are my master, my darling little god whom I am powerless to resist. If it pleases you to strike furious blows at my rump that you so love, take up the whip and strike, strike till you draw blood. I know you have been looking forward to that moment for a long time, it is something you have always wanted. It may be drawing near, but the ordeal is cruel, and weak my will.

When next we meet, I shall be your docile mistress with a voluptuous body, and you can love me dementedly.

Goodbye, my much loved, much cherished darling, this is a very long letter for you to read. I want a reply, do you hear? I will allow you to make it shorter but you will have plenty to talk about! I want to know all your thoughts, from the first day, I want to know whether you ever thought I was 'easy'. I gave in so quickly! You know you have been my only lover and that I adore you, but please release me from thinking about this.[17] I need our love to be pure.

---

17 We discover here that Simone is quite capable of lying. From reading the other letters in the briefcase, it is clear she had quite a few relationships before Charles. And years after their affair, she will be wonderfully deceitful again, when she tells her new lover that he is the only one she has ever spent such marvellous moments with and the only one she has ever loved.

Till Monday, my dear Charles. I love you and I now live only to keep our love going. I want it to be more beautiful than ever so that it can last a long, long time . . .

Goodbye, darling love. I am pressing my mouth to your hole and sucking it till I am quite out of breath.

I adore you.

Your Simone

Friday, midnight

My dear little Charles,
      Do forgive me for failing to write sooner but when I arrived yesterday morning I was immediately put to the grindstone and had an enormous amount of work. I wanted to come and talk to you yesterday evening but was too tired. I would not have written anything worth reading. You won't hold this twenty-four-hour delay against me, my love, will you?

I had a most charming journey and I am in a delightful spot. I shall be staying here at the Club; I have a large room which is very much like ours, my treasure (except for the looking glasses). You know, I have only one regret, and that is not having you by my side, knowing you are so far away! Why can we not escape all the obligations that keep us both prisoner? Why are you not free, my Charles? And could you not give me a few years of your life? I shan't say your whole life because I remember you once smiling when I said those words. It is when I am this far from you that I better appreciate everything you mean to me. And it is at times like this that all our memories come crowding into my mind. Then, my little one, I picture you as I love you best, tenderly passionate and as perverse as I could wish. This evening I am thinking of our most recent assignation, last Monday. Yes, we truly did surpass ourselves, we put extraordinary spirit into giving each other the wildest pleasures. My Lottie, you made me so happy giving yourself to me like that! Do you want to know how I feel when I take you like that? It can be summed up in three words: 'I go wild.' Yes, my love, when I feel your soft skin against mine, every ounce of me quivers, I quite lose my head and can think of only one thing: giving you pleasure, subjugating you with my fierce touch, taming your lascivious body and then taking that arse which I do so adore. Of course, I never forget it was thanks to me that you discovered the perversity of this coupling, and I am truly happy to see the glee with which you welcome it, and I shall always make love to you like that. I want to take you as wildly as I did on Monday. Once I am back I expect we shall have another hour together, my love, don't you think, and I shall prove just as filthy, just as perverted as last time. I shall hold you in my arms, my mouth will touch down onto your warm skin and I shall intoxicate you with almost imperceptible little kisses trailing all over your body. They will be like a breath of air, like a shiver. My lips will barely touch your skin, but it will thrill to such a sweet sensation. And my mouth will press itself to your mouth too. You will feel my tongue between your lips, and I shall keep yours prisoner for a long time while my hand reaches for your cock to pleasure it slowly.

Darling, I too cannot wait for our night of lovemaking. You will be loved to distraction, Lottie, for there will be nothing to stop us assuaging our tender feelings. I shall give you all the ministrations you love best. I shall kiss you and bugger you and nibble your cock and lick your balls, but, best of all, I shall give you the ardent sensations that fill both our dreams. Yes, it will make me immeasurably happy to initiate you to this new mystery, and it will afford me double the pleasure. We shall be very naughty indeed that night, my dear treasure. Before parting for many a long day, we shall love each other passionately so we can live off the memories while we are apart.

Like you, I hope the next photographs will be good. Yes, it will be terribly exciting to see them. What follies will you commit in Bandol with pictures like that to hand?

I cannot wait to come home, my dear treasure. Another two days, perhaps three, without seeing you. Are you sad when I am far away, and are you thinking of your little mistress, of your passionate, perverted lover?

Try to be free next Friday, my love, because I want you, I do want you so. I can no longer cope without you and your caresses, and I am dying to have you to myself, lying quite naked on the big divan where we have already committed such follies. I have a boundless longing for your whole body, I cannot stop thinking about it and I am very sad being so far from you. Yes, treasure, we shall have the most unforgettable times, for our ardour is far from extinguished and we love each other even more than before. The complete and total union of our bodies promises wonderful days ahead. Oh, quickly, quickly, come so I can love you, come and give me every inch of your soft skin for me to kiss.

Kissing you as tenderly as I love you. Goodbye again, dear little love god. Be good while I am away and try to be free on Friday so we can love each other with tireless energy. I am pressing my lips to your skin and kissing it passionately.

Simone

My dear love,

I am bored, I am so bored. I wish I were with you, close to you, the one I love. So many days have gone by since that wonderful hour when I held your beautiful body swooning in ecstasy in my arms! All I am left with is the ardent memory of it, and since then not once have my lips touched your skin.

Do you no longer want my body, my loved one? Do you no longer want the wild attentions that once afforded you such ecstasies? Have you already wearied of your lover's arms and do his ardent kisses kindle no response in you? Oh, how many hours have trickled by, my dear love, hours I have spent longing for your body! You will never know how thoughts of your soft flesh torment my nights alone, my nights without love or tenderness. Sometimes I wake and look for you beside me but, alas, I find only empty space, and your beloved name spills from my lips with all the loving words I send you.

My Lottie, my sweet mistress, how I love you! What sorcery, what secret spell do you use to hold my painful, tortured heart in your dear, dear hands? And what mysterious power there is in just one glance from you to make me love you more with each passing day! I have reached that stupid degree of love which reduces me to the level of a faithful dog, a big kind dog just waiting to be stroked by a much loved hand, living only to be petted by its master.

Oh, Charles, Charles. What sort of woman have you made of me? Do you at least understand how much I love you? I notice your every whim to please you. I anticipate anything that might be a pleasure for you, and I wish I could sweep aside every obstacle in your way, every petty woe which might impede your young god's progress. Oh my god, must I love you in order to want you so unrelentingly after thirteen months of passion?

When shall we have our next hour of lovemaking, darling? I have such a strong desire to take you lovingly and another, stronger still, to give myself to you, with all my heart. We shall probably now not have time to see each other again before the night you have been promising me for so long. I am not even sure whether we should see each other, for it will be very soon and we shall not have recovered from our letters. No, darling, let's wait, let's wait a little longer and the day will come when we can cleave to each other, brimming with desire and love. Oh, how I long for that night, how I look forward to it! How I shall love you, Lottie, when I have you in my arms. I shall dream up the rarest, sweetest embraces to intoxicate and arouse you, and your whole body will belong to me, completely, won't it, darling? Are you ready to submit to the ordeal I long to inflict on you? Are you ready to offer me your arse so the whip can leave its shrieking, smarting weals on you? My tongue and my 'prick' will be tireless in their efforts to make you forget that lacerating caress. I shall lavish you with pleasure. It will rise inside you in swift waves and you will not know how to resist it when you see that huge member probing deep into your flesh, oh yes, that member which my depravity chose specially for you.

And I know what voluptuous delights you in turn will give me. I am too aware of my lover's skill to doubt for one moment the pleasure I shall find in his arms. We shall bring our bodies together in the most adorable embraces. We shall become just one flesh, and the same spasm of delight will launch us both into the abyssal depths that leave us exhausted.

Oh, what a blissful image! I can see our bodies indistinguishable from each other, a tangle of limbs, and our mouths joined in an endless kiss which expresses all our tenderness. Do you not long for this hour of passion as I do?

My darling, my darling, my heart is full of you. If you only knew the fervour with which I pronounce your beloved name when I spend these lonely hours in misery, far from your arms! I study the little photograph of you and talk to it, describing all my pain, all my joy and all my hopes too. You are a constant part of my life, every minute of the day. I take you with me, guarding you jealously, and no one could guess the thoughts inside my head when my eyes drift off to the horizon. Dearly beloved darling, be happy, be proud. Isn't it wonderful to be loved like that? Oh, how I wish I could spoil you even more, my darling! I wish I could give you so many things, to make your life so pretty and peaceful, but there is an insurmountable obstacle between us and it forces me to be sensible. So I make do with the stolen hours, the moments that are, alas, only too brief, when you are partly mine as you were just now. Oh, my darling child, it was such a pleasure having you by my side! I wished our walk could go on and on, and we could run away together. Oh, Charles, I am so afraid of being hurt! How terribly you will make me suffer one day! Why did I give myself so utterly to you, given that the day will come when I shall have to take myself back? Put it off, my little Lottie, put it off as long as you can, for I shall be filled with vast sorrow the day when everything that was so beautiful ceases to exist.

Goodbye, beloved treasure, till tomorrow. Will you reply to this long letter? Surely you will. Tell me sweet things to calm me and soothe my pain. Tell me if you still love me as much, with the same love so dear to my heart. I want a very loving letter full of your tenderness, because you do still love me, don't you, Lottie darling?

Simone

My darling love,
    I have thought of you all day, and I have waited all day for this moment alone when I can at last write to you as I have been wanting to. When you arrive in Bandol tomorrow you will find the letter I wrote in terrible haste yesterday. Will you have written to me too, and will I have the pleasure of reading a few passionate pages?

And so now I am alone. My loved one, I am thinking of you, so far away, so very far away. And my heart constricts at the thought of all the hours I shall spend without you. I am a little sad, you know, and this separation, coming so soon after the first, weighs heavy on my heart which is so full of you.

How I love you, my dear darling! I cannot drive images of your dear self from my mind, and your name is constantly on my lips. You have captivated all of me with your touch and your kisses, and I am now yours, yours alone, do you know that? You have taken my whole heart away with you. Why did you not also take my body? Why must I be deprived yet again of this love which is my only joy?

In the silence of this stifling hot night, I conjure images of our last hours of pleasure, all our couplings, our every caress, and I can feel implacable desire for you rising through me, overwhelming me, making me restless and coursing feverishly in my veins. How clearly I see these arousing images, how eagerly I relive those delirious moments!

First things first, when we met the day after your return. A fortnight had passed, two whole weeks of waiting. At last I am with you again, I hold you to me. I have you there beside me, my Lottie, still just as beautiful and just as depraved, my adorable little mistress, my love. We take each other with demented ardour. Our bodies cleave tightly together, writhing to the same shudders, the same voluptuous delights. Do you know, the better hour in my view was the one we spent in your office? I waited for you with a beating heart, watching out for you, and soon you were in my arms with your lips on mine. Not wasting another moment, I kneel before you and my mouth takes hold of your stiffened prick, sucking it passionately. I lavish you with this touch you love, performing it wholeheartedly. I nibble your cock and you like it, I can tell, for I can feel him thrilling and pulsing between my teeth. He is hard, so hard, and I pause to gaze at this beautiful toy. Do you know you have a very beautiful cock and I love it?

May my letters sustain the sacred flame of desire in you to make you wilder and more loving than ever.

If I have a long letter tomorrow, I shall write straight away. I do not want to miss a single day of telling you how much I love you and how sad and lonely I feel when you are gone. I think of you all the time, and in my mind I relive all our wonderful loving moments.

Goodbye, my dear treasure, give me your lips for me to kiss, and give me your beloved eyes too.

I adore you. Write every day, my love.

Simone

M y darling Lottie,
         I received the long letter you wrote on Tuesday
in the three o'clock mail this afternoon, but have not
been able to answer it sooner. So I am writing to you now
from my little bedroom, behind closed doors, with your
dear photograph before my eyes, and you can peruse my
nakedness at your leisure, for I have nothing on at all
with this crushing heat.

I read your letter with great interest, my love, and I
shall be utterly open in answering the two questions you
asked.

I have never had a mistress before I met you, my little
Lottie, but I would be lying if I said I have never sought
out a woman. I wanted to have a taste of those wonderful
embraces which have been described to me a few times.
I dreamed of a gentle woman who might love me tenderly,
and I would certainly have returned the passionate attentions I hoped to receive from her. I always hesitated at
the last moment to embark on this adventure, held back
by obscure scruples, obscure prejudices, and I withheld
myself, hoping a better time might come. Should I regret
this virtuous past? Surely not, for it means I can now

say, 'Darling Lottie, you are my only mistress, my only sin, and I want to keep you forever because you give me the perverse sensations I so hoped to find.' I cannot know whether a woman might be more expert than a man, but I can assure you, my love, you have become a wonderful mistress and you make me immeasurably happy. You do not have to erase any memories from my body, but I will allow you to love me more wildly still so you need never fear that one day I might weary of you and leave you in order to renew my search for a woman. It is for you, my love, and you alone, to bind me to you forever. You know all my weaknesses, all my favourite sensations. Treat me to them lovingly and I shall never leave you, my beloved little Lottie.

It is a peerless pleasure feeling your tongue on my cunt. You suck it and lick it and draw it into your mouth. You imprison it with your lips and it is never long before I come. You can watch the mounting ecstasy on my face. My whole body contracts and in the final spasm I abandon myself entirely to the boundless intoxication of that exquisite touch. Be in no doubt, beloved girl, you are a talented mistress, and the pleasures you give me could not be bettered in the arms of another woman. My darling, you are allowing me to realise my dream to the full, and I adore you.

As for your second question, I am not sure what to say. I found it profoundly disturbing. Watching scenes of debauchery *with you*, seeing women sucking each other, and couples taking each other in the most outrageous positions . . . yes, it is very tempting, for I can imagine the orgies you and I would then enjoy, having been mutually aroused by such carnal sights. But I do wonder whether we need this new stimulant.[18] I do not think we do, my love. We have committed enough audacious acts ourselves to imagine what such scenes might be. What could we learn from them? Most likely nothing, but do tell me if it is what you want. Would you like to go and see such things, *with me* of course, for I do not think you would want to go alone or with someone else? We are quite mad, the pair of us, and I have no idea where this will all end.

No, my Lottie, I do not resent you for having this outlandish dream, and I love you more every day. Could I really resent you for such a small thing, particularly given the letters I write to you? I was afraid this dream might be masking a different desire and that you might want to taste those particular pleasures. But like you, dear beloved, I could not abide having a third person between us. I can barely tolerate the *legitimate* need to share your body. How could I cope if I had to surrender you to another mistress?

In fact, I wanted to ask you a question but you

---

18 There were no sex clubs in the modern sense of the term at this time in Paris, but there were lots of permissive establishments and brothels where orgies could take place.

pre-empted it by telling me I am your first male lover. Is that really true, and how did you develop this perverse wish to feel a male member inside you? I cannot believe I have corrupted you so and have such influence over you. In any event, I love you as you are, with your passions and your vices. I too wish we had the last plaything we need but, oh dear, how and where to find one? Do you have any ideas about this, darling Lottie? I think we shall have to settle for what we already have, and they do work wonders. When you come back, you just wait and see how I drive my ramrod up your arse, you filthy little pig. You can scream, I shall show no mercy and the bigger of the two will ply as deep as possible into your flesh. Twice I shall bugger you like that, three times if you have the strength, because it is what you truly crave and it makes me so happy seeing my Lottie completely aban-doning herself. Your arse presents itself to my phallus. It shudders, it writhes and every thrust of the hips makes you all the more mine. Push, darling, push hard. Come and get my big dick and let it give you the best climax. It does feel good, doesn't it, little pig, and oh you really do like that! Yes, you love being buggered, you little pervert, but I am here and I shall do it as much as you like. I really hope you never cast your eyes over men. That would be the end of you and me, for I want absolute ownership of your body as you do mine. I even wonder how I am not more outraged by the thought that you derive pleasure from the other woman. Everything you give to her is stolen from me, and I keep myself entirely for you. Is that fair, and why are you not free?

Yes, my dear love, I really do love being fucked by you now. True, in the early days of our affair I did not want to be subjected to this most banal of couplings but it now adds still more charm to our love. You are a remarkable lover. I cannot think how you do it but with you I have the wildest of climaxes, just from feeling your cock deep in me. What I do not want is for you to ejaculate in that position because that would lower us to the ranks of ordinary lovers. We know far more powerful sensations, but I want you to screw me relentlessly. I am not sure which position I prefer. Yes, your prick penetrates better when I am on my knees and you can fondle my rump and whip me from behind at the same time. But stomach to stomach, I feel I have full possession of your body and I can watch your cock driving in and out, and that is still more exciting. I shall put my arms around your back, holding you to me all the more tightly, and you will make me come for as long as you can hold back your own desire, then you can put your cock wherever you like for your passionate climax.

Oh, my darling treasure, it is so very long since we reached our ecstasy together! Since last we met and savoured such intense moments together, we have not had each other and yet we both feel such exasperating desire. I too can barely tolerate it any longer, my dear beloved. I am waiting impatiently till I see you again.

Only five more days now and then, I hope, I can give myself to you and take you too, my Lottie. Oh, I want you so much, my dear beloved little woman! My enchanting little mistress, I so desperately need your passionate embraces! Come quickly and slide your head between my thighs and lick my cunt unrelentingly. Empty it of its juices and let me taste them on your lips. And I want to suck your cock, kiss your arse and rub your balls, and most of all I want to bugger you, my love, to bugger you again and forever. There, right there, I'm taking you. Can you feel my rod in your hole? It drives in manically and I'm licking your skin. Again, again, give yourself, give yourself up.

I hope I can see you on Tuesday the 17th. It definitely will not be in the morning. I shall telephone you to arrange it. It will be in the afternoon; I have no idea what time, most likely at five o'clock. I shall do everything I can but it will be difficult for me to get away much in the next two weeks because of moving house. Still, we must not despair and, anyway, we have the whole winter ahead to be together, my beloved, don't we? What do our difficulties matter if we can see each other for an hour or two every week? We have faith in each other now, don't we, and surely our love is strong enough to withstand anything, even absence? I love you madly, my dear darling, and I am yours, you do know that, don't you?

You can keep me as long as you like, my dear treasure. You have captured me indefinitely with your wonderful caresses, and I adore you. It is getting late, darling Lottie. Goodnight. I shall go to sleep thinking passionately of you, darling. I offer you my whole body. Take it in a wild embrace to exhaust us both and connect us forever.

Till tomorrow, my love, my mouth on your beloved lips.

Simone

Having already admitted that she 'dreamt of a gentle, lascivious mistress', Simone once again reveals her lesbian tendencies. Was this an unusual leaning in 1929 France? Sapphism was in fact not only widespread but also very much in fashion, if not throughout France, at least in Paris, particularly in wealthier circles. This was due to the dramatic increase in all forms of pleasure-seeking in the aftermath of the First World War, and was true throughout Europe, in Berlin even more so than in Paris. Millions of young men had died in the war. Women, who had taken over men's roles in industry and agriculture alike while their men were at the front, were now claiming their emancipation. The year 1922 saw the publication of Victor Margueritte's book La Garçonne, *featuring an androgynous and rebellious young woman who characterised the 1920s. She is not necessarily homosexual, but she takes it upon herself to dismiss feminine traits and assume masculine ones. Trousers, jackets and ties started to appear in women's clothing. In the space of a few short years, hems rose from the ankle all the way up to the knee. Women's hair was cut short and the top designers, starting with Chanel, rode on this wave right through to the Second World War. At the time, Paris had many establishments – such as the famous Monocle – reserved exclusively*

for women. Society continued to ostracise male homo-
sexuality, while on the other hand displaying a degree
of tolerance to Sapphic practices. As these women were
not persecuted for their sexual orientation, they felt little
need to rally themselves, and it would be false to refer
to any 'lesbian identity' as a social body at the time; in
fact, it is highly likely that plenty of women who felt
drawn to their own sex didn't even know the term, or
at least didn't use it, which is why we don't find it in
Simone's writing. Women with this leaning – and Proust
talks about them at length – would have witnessed many
prominent figures who didn't hide their tastes; the Paris-
based American Gertrude Stein, for example, had
considerable influence on the intellectual scene of the
day. It is therefore quite understandable that Simone
should disclose unapologetically to her lover about this
additional 'vice'.

Saturday morning

My dear beloved,

This morning I received the letter you wrote on Thursday. I did not go to the office yesterday afternoon. I hope the letter I posted on Thursday evening reached you in Narbonne.

The four pages I have just read made me very happy, my dear friend. That is how I love you best, when you can describe all our passionate moments, and were it not for the separation, I would frequently send you to Bandol. You are subject to no outside influences there, no embraces from anyone other than me, and you are all mine. I am happy then, my dear love, for I can feel how loving and passionate you are, and I know my letters ignite boundless desire in you, and your longing is intensified. You must also notice how tender I make my letters. Just like you, I let my heart speak so these letters carry a bit of me in them for you. I too wait impatiently for the post to arrive, and devour the pages you send me with great joy.

But I must scold you today, beloved Lottie. Whatever sort of outlandish idea has inveigled its way into your head, and what makes you think I wish I had the mistress

I once dreamed of meeting? Why do you doubt my tenderness is exclusive? My dear love, do you not know you have replaced every single mistress I could possibly have desired? Do you not know that in your arms I live the most intense experiences whose memory can never be erased from my mind? Oh, my Lottie, why do you think I would ask a woman, however beautiful, for the caresses you administer so well? When you hold my cunt's little button between your hot lips, when you suck it and lick it, do you not soon feel a rush of sperm flowing into your mouth, and can you not read in my expression the boundless pleasure you have just given me? Believe me, my dear friend, you make me happier than I can express, and you allow me to realise my wildest dreams. No, I would never leave you for a woman, I would never give my cunt to a mistress, for I love you too much to contemplate such a thing for one moment. I have given myself to you without reservations, you know that; I have put my every hope in your hands, and you alone will decide the day we part. I still have too much love in me, my loved one, to think of looking for new sensations elsewhere. You are my lover whom I adore. I surrender myself to you with infinite tenderness, and you have never disappointed me. I have always been absurdly happy in your arms. You have succeeded in binding me to you with ties even stronger than love: with the ties that originate in my flesh, in the very depths of my being, and you would have to hurt me terribly to tear them apart. If you want to carry on surrounding me with your tenderness like this, if you want to give me the same caresses, we could stay together for a long time to come. There is only one thing I crave, my big boy, and that is to be back in your arms in our hideaway, and to shower you unstintingly with every proof of love you want from me.

I now know the incredible sensation that you dream of having. On your return I shall re-enact what I did in my office last Thursday. You will present me with your magnificent arse which I so love. Once I have prepared it with my expert kisses, I shall drive my huge prick into you. Your flesh stretches and gleams. What a perfect place for my tongue! While I bugger you with my cock, my deft tongue licks the flesh around your hole. Under the effects of this perverse caress, you shudder peculiarly and I can feel your hardened cock pulsing in my hand. Is that how you want me to love you, my dear love? Tell me soon.

You could not have made me happier than you did by saying you love screwing me. We really are two little pigs. We have finally succeeded in uniting our vices to make us truly happy, and many an intense hour together still lies in store for us. I have just been given the letter you sent from Tarascon on Friday. What a lovely surprise, my darling, and how happy I am! But once again you have brought up a subject which I am beginning to find difficult, for I now wonder whether it is in fact you who wants this other mistress, so you can watch her fucking me and sucking me before your eyes. If your dream had such an effect on you, then it must have given you a great deal of pleasure. So, Charles, would you like it if I took such liberties in front of you, and delighted in another woman's touch? Can you picture me on the bed in another mistress's arms, giving her the attentions I lavish on you, or taking her between my thighs and showering my juices into her mouth? You are making me unhappy, for I am beginning to doubt whether, despite what you say, I alone can satisfy all your cravings. Do you think you could enjoy a threesome? Would you tolerate having another woman between us? I could not, you can be sure of that. I never could. Tell me honestly. *I want to know* why you keep talking about this. I shall say once again that you are everything to me and you make me very happy; where would I find a mistress with not only your tongue but also your cock? No, my darling, I want no other lover but you. Don't leave me. If I am not sufficiently depraved to pleasure you, tell me, I shall try to become even more so, but I do not want to lose you, nor to share you again. I could never love a mistress in front of you. No, no. What madness to think it!

When you are back we shall meet as soon as I am free and, my dear beloved, you will see how fervently I can love you. Oh, I too long to be reunited with your wonderful body, I want to smother it with rabid kisses and press my skin against yours. My Lottie, I want you to take me in a never-ending coupling, and then I shall be your passionate male lover. Together we shall know exactly how to replace a third mistress. You will suck my cunt while, at the same time, I suck your cock. You will bugger me and I will bugger you at the same time. We can do that, can we not?

Write soon to tell me I alone am mistress of your body, that you are happy with my kisses and you asked this outlandish question to test my love. But no, tell me nothing but the truth.

I shall try to write again before Monday but we shall be back in Paris this evening. You should have received a letter when you reached Narbonne. Write soon. I beg you. Not long now, dear love. My wildest caresses all over you, everywhere.

Your Simone

Saturday evening

My darling Lottie,
I dropped in at the office at five o'clock and was thrilled to find the letter you wrote on Thursday. You must have found a lot of mail in Narbonne to make you forget the day's disappointment. I am waiting impatiently for your latest letters, my love, for they will tell me you are heading back to me and I shall at last be able to prove my tender feelings for you, and they are immeasurable.

Oh, my darling, there is no need for a third person between us. Have we not conjured the astonishing impression of two extra lovers?[19] We are so happy together, my treasure, why would we want to share that happiness? You asked me to tell you how I love you. Do you not know, my beloved? Can I explain it any more emphatically? Darling little Lottie, don't you know you make me deliriously happy? Don't you know that in you I have found the adorable mistress I longed to find? And now I ask nothing more than the possibility of keeping you forever. Could I love another woman? No, darling, I am quite sure I could not. You are too deeply embedded

---

19 Here, Simone evokes the two 'aids'.

in my being, not only in my flesh but also in my heart, for it to occur to me to look for anything more than I already receive from you. Do you not yet realise, when I have been saying it for so long, that I have a deep and unwavering passion for you, and that my only purpose in life is to keep your love which makes all my dearest wishes come true? If you love me as much, I feel sure we can prolong our idyll . . . But is your love that strong?

In my case, I am not the only woman in your life, you must not forget that, darling. You often have to share your attentions and your kisses, and I hope you can see that this is of huge significance, for I shall never be the only love in your heart and your senses. If you loved me to the same extent as I do you, you simply could not accept the touch of other lips or contact with another body. It seems impossible and yet you did once admit to me that you find pleasure in those arms which are not mine. A lesser pleasure perhaps, but you still derive enjoyment from caresses other than mine. Do you know, I cannot even bring myself to think of this however hard I try, and it pains me more than you can imagine? Oh, my Lottie, if I did not love you so help-lessly, what harm could your wife's existence do me? I met you when you were not free, and still agreed to be your mistress. At the time, I confess, I did not think of her. But over these fifteen months, now that you have become the only thought in my head, now that I have a deeper appreciation of the treasure trove that is your body, I cannot reconcile myself with sharing you. I can always feel her there between us; I shall never succeed in replacing her for you. She is the last link keeping you from me, and it is an invincible link.

That is how much I love you, Charles. I love you so much that this situation which I have to accept affords me terrible suffering. In order to keep you, I must tolerate this other woman and suffer, or if I am not to suffer I must relinquish you. Well, I prefer to suffer and to keep you. Would you do as much? If you really love me as you say you do, if you love me so much you do not want another man to have the pleasure of my body, you must understand what I am saying and you must pity me.

My darling Lottie, do you now truly know that I love you? Do you now truly know that I have only one wish, to keep you like this forever? Yes, I want you to create the disturbing illusion that you are a woman. In the darkness of our room when I touch your tiny little breasts and your smooth pure chest, I can already believe you are the same sex as me. Even your hips and stomach are those of an adorable woman, and your skin is so soft it makes my head swim. And when your tongue sucks at my cunt with unparalleled ardour, I forget everything and give myself entirely to you. Yes, you certainly are the ardent mistress I dreamed of meeting, and you are a very obliging pupil. But if you want to experiment with this, we shall try. You can make your prick and balls disappear between your thighs. All that is left between your hips will be your curly brown pelt, then you will be completely like a woman, and I will bring my mouth to it lovingly as I would to my mistress's cunt.

Oh, my beloved little Lottie, how I long to savour your ardent, passionate touch once more! I want to be back in your arms, exploring your voluptuous body, holding it to me to warm my heart with the heat of your satiny skin. I cannot wait to swoon with delight. My every waking moment is spent in anticipation of your return, which is now so soon. And, my darling lover, I also dream of your beautiful cock, knowing you will ply him skilfully into my cunt, into my arse, into my mouth and between my breasts. Yes, would you like that? I am shivering all over at the thought of the countless ecstasies I shall have in your arms. Our little room will be the site of demented orgies, my treasure, for what follies we shall commit when we are reunited after so long an absence! We shall avenge ourselves for the cruel waiting imposed on our mutual desire, and for the enforced chaste behaviour we have both had to endure.

Yes, we really are filthy, my love, but oh, what pleasure we have! We have experimented with every perverse delight and kept those we liked best. I think there is nothing we do not now know about the secrets of love-making, for we have spent fifteen months climbing the rungs of the ladder of vice with alarming poise. I would say we have nothing left to learn, my treasure. What more could we do in a year's time? I cannot think, but there is most likely nothing, unless between now and then you manage to convince me and we have found a delicious girlfriend who might agree to watch our couplings and participate in them. But why should I not find a male lover just as passionate as you, who could give you the feeling you still want? A gorgeous, well-endowed boy who could bugger you or whose prick I could suck. Wouldn't you like that, Lottie? We can discuss it again, all right? I myself would rather that than a woman, because I could be buggered by you at the same time. Then you would have twice the pleasure, do you see?

In the meantime, I hope we have not come to that, for it would be the end of our love. If one of us were to need another lover, it would mean our passion was dead, for at present we are perfectly happy together, at least I believe we are.[20]

On Tuesday then we shall probably be free to love each other frenziedly and the thought makes me tremble all over with desire. Oh, my Lottie, it will be so good to see you again after such a long absence, and with all my

---

20 It is unlikely that Simone is keen to have a threesome of any kind. Her main objective is to avoid at any cost seeing Charles with another woman; she is even jealous of women who happen to be travelling in the same train carriage as him! But she knows that keeping Charles means continuing to provide more unexpected pleasures. This is why she tries to persuade him to include a man in their adventures, a proposal she suspects Charles will never take up.

appetites enervated by this fasting. I am sure we shall spend a magical hour together, just like last time which left us with such lasting memories.

Come to me quickly, my beloved darling, and give me every inch of your thrilling flesh. Come quickly and nestle in my arms. I want to kiss your adorable body, I want to make your cock harden and your little arse quiver. I shall suck your hole with such ardour, my Lottie, and lick your cock too, and soon your sperm will jet out, spraying over my lips and breasts.

And you, come and kiss my cunt, suck my button, and bugger me too, my filthy little darling. Screw me and spank me. I shall spill all my juices over your cock. I must leave you now, my darling, but I shall see you on Tuesday. I shall telephone your office at about 11.30, and I hope that a few hours later we shall at last be able to meet in our little room, and love each other passionately for an hour.

Goodbye, darling little Lottie, I adore you more than anything else. Please don't ever talk again about subjecting me to another woman, I really do not want that. And you, do you want another lover with a magnificent prick? Is your current lover who adores you so much no longer enough for you?

Till Tuesday, my beloved one. I hope your balls are bursting and your cock is hard so you can screw me and bugger relentlessly. I adore you.

Simone

Darling love,

One day follows another but alas they are so different. This time yesterday we were together in our blissfully private little nest, making love to each other passionately. All the follies we committed have left me with the voluptuous aches and cramps that follow love-making, and my exhaustion is very dear to me, for it sustains the memory of your ardent kisses.

Today I only glimpsed you in passing but that brief moment was enough to last me a whole day. And I am still thinking of you, of us, with the same ardour, and the same tenderness.

My dear darling, do you realise everything you gave me yesterday? Do you know you satisfied my wildest desires more fully than ever, and I left your arms drained, spent, empty, with both my head and my heart aching from the full force of your embraces? My dear love, how could you think I might forget you with such exploits? How could you think I might tear myself away from your arms to look elsewhere for delusory caresses which could never match yours? So long as you love me, my dear darling, I shall love you and I shall have no greater happiness than continuing to be your faithful and passionate mistress, do please believe me. It is up to you alone to keep me forever. Darling, do you want to love me as I love you? Do you want us to prolong the delicious dream we have been enjoying for almost sixteen months? Every day brings us closer, my dear loved one, and our desire for each other is just as violent as it was in the first month of our affair. In you I have found the most entrancing of mistresses and the most loving of men. You play both roles with peerless mastery and, whether you are a man or a woman, the sublime sensations I have in your arms bind me to you more violently with every embrace.

Yesterday you made me believe you were an adorable little woman, do you know that? Yes, perhaps you don't realise, you truly were my little Lottie. I muttered that name passionately in the ardent moments when you made me climax, and that is the best proof that you have succeeded in being as lifelike as possible, if I can forget your original sex and believe I am in the arms of a passionate mistress.

You were my little woman. Yes, I am going back over the scene in minute detail. First you sucked my cunt with astonishing ardour. With your head between my thighs, you squeezed my tingling button between your lips and I sucked your balls and stroked your firm rump and the supple small of your back, and I climaxed wildly to your devastating touch.

You soon took me in your arms and drove a spectacular member into me. You leaned over me, affording the sight of your adorable little breasts, pointing their pink nipples towards my mouth. I reached out a hand to them lovingly and they quite filled it, and my fingers fondled these enchanting toys which I adore. I knew so little about those dear small breasts, but yesterday I came to know them and the illusion was quite complete. It was no longer Charles who was kissing me passionately but Lottie, my divine little Lottie who had equipped her virgin hips with an impressive dildo to please me, and she drove it boldly into my cunt. My dear love, I have lost count of how many times you made me come. You went beyond my expectations and surpassed yourself. Showing extraordinary skill which I had not suspected in you, you managed to make me accept your cock in my cunt for many a long minute, and I who was once indifferent to this banal coupling, I who forbade it from the first day of our romance, can no longer survive without it.

You brought me to a devastating climax, my loved one, and now I cannot stop thinking of that complete union of our beings which makes me so intensely happy.

You see, darling, we shall soon need the wonderful toy we dream of having. Given that my suggestion does not appeal to you, given that you do not want me to find a handsome, well-endowed lover for you, I want you to use me to create the illusion for you. For almost a year now I have managed to bugger you every time we have been together, but I know how far from real the sensations I give you are. And that upsets me terribly, for I should really like to be the wonderful, tireless male lover whose memory would dog your thoughts day and night.

My dear love, have you thought what my embraces would be like if I had an impressive member strapped around my middle and a magnificent pair of balls between my legs? It would be easy for me to change sex, and then I could lie down on the bed and offer you my stiff cock which you could take into your avid mouth while you stroked my beautiful balls.

Once you are truly aroused by these ministrations, I would lovingly straddle your body and wrap my strong arms around you, I would bugger you with my big dick, plying it into you up to the balls. And you are most likely aware that these devices can create the even more extraordinary illusion of sperm being discharged. A bit of warm water is all it takes to replace that sublime liquor which I should like to see flowing freely between your buttocks.

I can already imagine the astonishing positions we shall adopt. And I am sure you will then be mine forever, for I shall no longer be afraid of anyone. You will be left drained by my spirited attentions manifested in still more audacious ministrations than I give you now. I adore you, you know that, and I want to give you maximum pleasure so that it never even occurs to you to leave me. Who could take possession of your ardent flesh better than me, my Lottie, tell me that? If you want, you can give me the means to take it still more fully, and then you will see what a wonderful man I can become for you.

I shall leave you to think about this idea and some day soon you yourself will probably strap a monstrous prick around my middle so that it can drive all the way into your intimate flesh which I do so adore, just as yours did into me yesterday.

I know you like being buggered, I know this more fully than you do yourself, for no one can feel as I do the way your flesh contracts around my tongue. And I know with a dildo like that you would have the hallucinatory sensations afforded by a beautiful male cock voluptuously discharging into your arse.

And I too could satisfy my passion by fucking myself ardently without fear of tiring you with successive couplings.

I want no other mistress and you want no other man. My darling, we love each other enough to use all the means at our disposal to achieve whatever excesses these third parties might do for us, don't you think?

Yes, together we shall act out scenes of debauchery, perhaps this winter. Our depravity is becoming all-consuming, I can feel it. We shall never escape its clutches. But surely that depravity is the only reason our union is so lasting? Without it, we would have wearied of the usual ministrations, thanks to it we are bound to each other and nothing could separate us but a mutual loss of interest. But we are finding more pleasure than ever together, and only yesterday I realised that everything is still just as ardent as at the start of our romance.

But I want you to belong to me even more fully, my darling love. I want to take you relentlessly, and I shall work at that with the full force of my tenderness, which is boundless.

Yes, starting on Monday, we can see each other every evening and that makes me very happy, for I could not go on any longer apart from you, my tender darling. I should like to thank you from the bottom of my heart for thinking of escorting me home every evening, for I was sad to think we might not be able to spend just a few, alas very brief, moments alone together.

There, my loved one, this is a very long letter. Shall I have a reply on Monday evening? I shall telephone on Monday morning when I arrive at the office. I adore you and send you passionate kisses, my entrancing little Lottie.

Simone

M y dear beloved,
    You must be arriving in Nice as I write, after a good journey, I hope.

Meanwhile, I am alone, desperately alone under rainy skies which are chilling my poor heart! I was already feeling very sad, and this morning I carried out a painful duty. I went to the graveyard with a friend of mine (you know, the 'woman with the turban'). The man she has been with for ten years has died. She had to wait till the 'other woman' (because alas there is also an 'other woman') had left the graveside before she could say her final farewell! What a dismal task it was giving my poor friend support. And what a painful situation is ours, the mistresses who live in the margins of your lives, when you are the ones we adore! I am not very cheerful, my dear beloved, as you can see. But how could I be when I feel such pain, such pain inside?

My little one, my darling whom I love, why did you leave me, even if only for a week? You obviously don't know the emptiness you leave behind. And yet you do know, for I never stop telling you I love you! Especially as yesterday we were together. Once more the door closed behind us, and we gave ourselves to each other with the same insatiable desire. Yesterday I held your adorable body in my arms! Do you remember, my dear treasure? You read my letter avidly, with your cock already rearing with ardent longing. My mouth sucked at it lovingly and my swift, deft tongue ran from your balls to its red head. I dotted kisses all along your member. And you had a formidable erection. Then, turning to your arse, I had the audacity to push the tip of my big pink nipple into it! I pleasured you with that little button. I think it even went a little way inside! My tongue also probed your thrilling flesh and you were already climaxing.

I have relived our heavenly embraces in my dreams and I saw your dick imprisoned between my breasts again. I made a necklace of warm flesh for him, and you rubbed back and forth between my breasts while I pushed them together, then a jet of sperm drenched me and I spread it all over my breasts, much to your delight!

Tell me soon how you felt about this new way of finding pleasure, my dear beloved. Did you savour it fully? Tell me, was it 'dirty' enough watching that pink head emerging from my opulent globes? And when your come squirted out, oh the glow of debauchery in your swooning eyes! Which coupling do you like best, tell me? You know plenty now! You have come right down my throat, you have offloaded in my big arse, you have tugged yourself off before my eyes and you have drenched my body with your come. Lastly, yesterday, you inaugurated this new method which, I think, did not displease you! Which will you choose next time? Tell me soon, my dear treasure!

Another appalling week to get through far from you, far from your arms! I am so sad at the thought of heading off alone every evening without you by my side! I have grown so accustomed to our daily ritual that I have no idea how to organise my life if I don't see you! This evening I shall rush home early for I have the most terrible chagrin to overcome. I shall slink off to a quiet corner of the house and reread your last two letters, while I wait to receive more!

My dear love, don't abandon me, don't leave me. If you knew just how utterly I am yours you would understand my isolation. You are everything to me. Apart from you, I have nothing to love like that. Swear to me that you still love me just as much, tell me, my dear treasure!

I was happy you allowed me to come and see you yesterday evening, even though I was sad to watch you leave. Did I not have your last kiss, your last smile, your last wave? Ah! How I love you, how I do love you. A love like that cannot possibly ever end, and you will always be a part of me, for you are *my first, my true love!* Nothing before you counts. After you? Ah! Better not to think yet about after you, for it would be so devastating if you ever said anything final that it makes me shudder from head to foot. Yes, it would have to come from you. You yourself would suffer so little that I would have no regrets. Can a man suffer? No, and anyway, are we not here to pick up the injured bird?

Whereas, can you see, it would be abysmal for me? Oh, my loved one, come back soon and clasp me to you in a wonderful embrace. Come back soon to take relentless possession of my body which yields to your caresses! Look, I am waiting for you. I am naked under the covers, with my thighs spread as they were yesterday. Come and fuck me, my dear love, come quickly! Oh yes, that's good like that. Make me come, make me come. I spray all my come over your cock, you darling bastard. Is it good, tell me, is it good?

Ah! No, there is nothing to compare to the intensity of that coupling. And to think that for sixteen months I scorned it! But you will help me make up for lost time, won't you, dear beloved, and that is how you will love me from now on.

I also hope I shall soon have a long letter from you! Let your heart speak, my love, given that you love me! You know how charming I find your sweet tender words, and how happy I am when I read your letters. Tell me what I mean to you, and how much pleasure it gives you taking my depraved body! What ministrations am I best at giving you, my beloved darling?

I shall write without fail tomorrow and on Saturday I shall probably be able to reply to your letter! Tell me when you will be back, my loved one, and if you are utterly and completely adorable you will let me know what time you will arrive so I can come to collect you.

You granted me the sadness of your leaving, tell me, won't you grant me the joy of your return? Goodbye, my big darling boy, I shall stop now, till tomorrow! Will you cast a quick eye over my big arse this evening before you go to sleep? Come back as soon as possible, for I long to see you again, my loved one. And write me a letter or two, I'm so lonely!

Sending passionate kisses to every inch of your glorious body! Be good, stay faithful to me for a week at least!!!

I adore you, my dear darling.

Simone

My darling love,
        Two more hours and I shall finally set off to be reunited with you. I really cannot wait to kiss your beloved lips passionately, and time goes so slowly without you.

I have been incredibly preoccupied since this morning, my loved one, because when I woke I was still caught up in my dream from last night and I just cannot shake off the thought of it.

Listen . . .

We were in a huge apartment, me, you and another young man. We were drinking copious amounts of champagne and the three of us were naked. You started stroking me lovingly, your cock straining with violent longing, while our friend sucked furiously at your arse. All of a sudden you were lying full length on some cushions and he was sucking your cock while I pleasured him vigorously with my hand. Meanwhile, you had your head between my thighs, drinking my free-flowing juices.

Then you turned and reciprocated the attention on him. His glorious prick disappeared between your lips and I pleasured your cock just as powerfully as I had his, while I plied my cunt with my other hand.

Then he and I set each other a challenge, to be the one to make you come. Who would do it best? So next came this extraordinary scene: our young friend drove his rigid prick into you, and I watched him buggering you. I was crazed with jealousy but you did not come under his brutal attentions. And then I noticed an enormous dildo under the table. I picked it up and immediately started buggering you with it myself. I kept my stomach pressed up against your arse and drove the magnificent member into your hole while my hand worked expertly on your prick. You shuddered strangely and did not ask for mercy. Twice, three times I took you like that, and soon you collapsed onto the divan, overwhelmed.

I woke this morning very disturbed by this outrageous dream and have not stopped thinking about it since. I want to make it come true, when can I? Let's talk about it this evening, can we?

I adore you, my loved one, I shall see you soon, but I want your arse all to myself, and not be forced to give it to anyone else . . . unless that really is what you want!

Simone

My great love,

Before anything else you must forgive this morning's letter and tear it up. I do not want to leave any trace of my absurd jealousy which suddenly erupts despite my best efforts. I want to stop tormenting you, my dear darling, and although, alas, I may continue to suffer, you will hear no more of my heart's laments, and you can believe I am finally cured of this evil which gnaws at me stealthily. Yes, I have faith in you, I have faith in your love, and I ask only one thing, that you keep your softest caresses and your wildest embraces for me, and when you are in my arms you are the depraved and passionate lover I have created for myself, and for myself alone.

I adore you, my dear love, you are my whole life, and my body will know no other touch but yours. So long as you love me, I shall be yours, I swear it.

Will tomorrow be the day we can be together at last, when we can melt into each other in one of those couplings which drains us by so utterly fulfilling us? I can feel an imperious craving for your body rising within me, and I want to love you more wildly than ever. These long days apart have whipped all my senses into a paroxysm of longing, and I can tell I shall throw myself on you tomorrow, succumbing to the full ardour of my desire. And, darling, you will give me that beautiful body which I adore. I have not laid eyes on it for a week, and I have a burning need to smother it with delirious kisses.

I am not yet sure how this sensational hour will end. How would you like to come, my love? Shall I provide a warm haven for your cock between my breasts? Would you like me to swallow your come? Or will you bugger your darling little bitch? Or perhaps you will pleasure your beautiful prick before her eyes and sully her swooning body with hot, cloying sperm. We cannot predict that final moment, and we can decide nothing in advance, for it will all depend on what powers of resistance we have tomorrow after an hour of demented couplings. We shall be truly exhausted but I shall still have the strength to make you offload furiously. You must tell me how you want me to take you, with my breasts, my mouth or my arse, and I shall give myself entirely to you.

You must love me with all your might, Charles, to prove that your desire is as keen as it always has been, and that you are deliriously happy in my arms.

I am waiting impatiently for our tryst when I can make you offload uncontrollably. I have never been such a dirty bitch as I am now, and my longing for you is wilder than ever. You will discover that for yourself tomorrow.

I am alone in the little room where we once loved each other so frenziedly, do you remember, and as I write, I am stroking my button with one firm finger, and I can feel it swelling and preparing to climax. A boundless exhilaration steals over my whole body, and I would finish the deed if I did not plan to save all this come, and give it to you tomorrow. You will make it spray out with your skilled tongue, and your cock will find every last drop in the depths of my cunt, won't it, my darling love? You will fuck me furiously, and my thighs are spreading of their own accord at the thought of the wonderful sensations you give me. Oh, I love you, you are an incomparable lover and I want to keep you forever and ever.

Till this evening, my beloved love, but even more so, till tomorrow. I adore you, dear lover. Fuck me hard.

Simone

Very unusually, this last letter is dated – 14 November 1929. This dating could possibly be explained by the fact that this is an anniversary of sorts: the letter comes seventeen months after Simone's affair with Charles began (we know from a previous letter that they met on 14 June 1928), so perhaps, miscalculating, Simone had this marked as their year and a half anniversary. This is an indication of the extreme importance Simone attaches to the passage of time endorsing a relationship which she knows is fragile.

This is three weeks after the Crash of 1929, which was to throw Europe into chaos and launch mankind towards the Second World War; but Simone is not concerned with outside events. Her only focus of interest is her relationship with Charles, and her correspondence reveals only fragmentary snatches of her life, confining itself to this all-consuming passion.

My loved one,

 You will not be surprised to hear I was filled with emotion when I reread the letter I had skimmed through all too quickly in your presence. Deciphering those perverse and passionate words a second time ignited such feverish desire that I was unable to get to sleep until well into the night. Unfortunately, it was impossible for me to assuage my rutting senses, for the current arrangements forbid me any freedom. Besides, I prefer it thus, for tomorrow I shall give you all the reserves of vigorous longing I have within me, and it will be your fierce kisses that make me die with pleasure.

 So, my dear love, you have agreed to accept the ultimate experience I dream of providing for you. Yes, I confess, such a scene would be a tempting sight for the passionate mistress that I am, and I feel sure it will afford me a rare delight to see you succumbing to the assaults of a valiant male. But you know, to achieve this we shall need an evening of pure madness, an evening when we are both inflamed and overexcited . . . For I am still not sure I would have the strength to surrender you to anyone in cold blood. I promised I would let you have this perverse sensation, but I cannot make up my mind. One evening when you are free, completely free, we shall go together to find a handsome lover worthy of taking your thrilling body, and before my eyes you will offer up your arse to his hard cock. I can picture the scene in astonishing detail: the man is lying quite naked. You suck avidly at his limp cock which soon responds to your ardent kisses and rears its proud head, and when it is perfectly ready, you then take his place. You lie your glorious body down on the bed. Resting your head between your arms and with your thighs raised, you reach your little brown hole towards this muscular male. He straddles your body and, gripping your shoulders the better to hold his prey, he gives one brutal thrust and drives his triumphant member into your vanquished flesh. He's buggering you, my Charles, this handsome lover you have dreamed of finding is buggering you, and you can feel his full round balls knocking between your thighs. Your body contracts and shudders to this devastating sensation. I have at last allowed you to realise your wildest longing, and I welcome back into my arms a lover exhausted and conquered, still gasping from his extraordinary climax.

Darling Charles, you must understand how much I adore you if I am prepared to give you this proof of my love. You must understand how much I long to please you if I consent to this outlandish idea: giving you a male lover. And I wonder anxiously whether you will develop too keen a liking for this coupling and will want to repeat it in future. But no, that won't happen, will it, dear darling? And you will come back to me with the same tenderness you have shown me for eighteen months. I trust in your love, and I believe all the sweet things you say in your letter.

If you love the depraved mistress you have in me, if you love her above all else, I am not afraid of disappointing you, because my own desire for you is more violent than ever. I long night and day for that glorious body of yours, and I picture its every secret contour. Your adorable little breasts with their pink nipples, your smooth white stomach, the dark curls jealously guarding the pink flower of your cock, and lastly but best of all your hole in all its mystery, the part I love most. Darling, you cannot imagine the happiness I feel when I take possession of that warm flesh which gradually gives way to my tongue's wilful probing, and my pleasure knows no bounds when I drive my prick between your taut buttocks.

Yes, give me this wonderful plaything soon. Gird my hips with the fearsome cock and you will soon see that you can already have the most exquisite sensations in my arms. Who knows, I may even manage to match the possible lover I plan to offer you. In any event, I know you will wait more patiently for this new exploit, for I shall be sure to bind you irresistibly to me when I take total possession of your flesh as I have done in the wildest dreams that fill my titillated mind. Yes, dear love, for a year now I have been the indefatigable male lover your depravity craved, and I shall always want to be, if that is what you want too. When you have given me the impressive dildo, I will have nothing left to fear and you will surrender yourself to me completely and utterly. No, I will not try out my powers on another mistress. Have I not found in you the most entrancing and fervent of girlfriends? Do you not give me every pleasure I crave, and are you not a docile plaything who accepts my every whim?

I have not forgotten the indelible experiences we had last week. With your little pink breasts quivering in my hand, you are the most beautiful mistress I could wish for, and I want you alone. You are my beloved little woman, my Lottie whom I adore, and I have such wonderful experiences in your arms that I shall always remember them. You have become very adept in the art of sucking my cunt, and I have no doubt you will find ways to do better still. Has it occurred to you that with the dildo you will be able to screw me tirelessly? The illusion will then be complete for me because you will be disguising your true sex, revealing it only at the last moment when, helplessly aroused by the frenzied attentions you have lavished on me, you can no longer contain your desire.

My dear love, tomorrow we shall meet again in our lovely big room. And I know we shall be filthier than ever for we shall be picturing these future scenes of debauchery. I shall play the part of that unknown man for you. I shall take your conquered flesh furiously, and you will be my little Lottie, my ardent and depraved little woman.

Tomorrow I should like to experience the sensation you have described. You can bugger me and trail your tongue all around my hole. And I shall return to licking both your cock and your arse. Your flesh will have to relax considerably to accommodate my huge prick. And you will suck me relentlessly, and fuck me as, before your eyes, I fondle myself as I do when I am alone and you will be doubly aroused.

Ah! Darling, what else shall we invent to afford still wilder pleasures? We are sinking ever deeper into our depravity as if into quicksand from which there is no escape. Shall we reach the depths of this unsuspected abyss together, a place where our very sanity wavers and our free will surrenders, and shall we one day be united by still more unusual pleasures? I do hope so, my love, for we are irresistibly bound by this depravity. Our intertwined bodies are sliding down the slope and we cannot stop this descent by clinging to any branch. That fragile branch was modesty, but we snapped it long ago and we now scatter its twigs around us with every new fall. Do you want to slip into that bottomless abyss with me? Do you love me enough to attempt the journey? Are you afraid of my depravity? Are you afraid that our shared madness should become your own madness? Will you ever be able to erase the stigmata of my love from your body? No, you have now been stamped with my seal. You belong to me and I shall keep you. I shall take you to a fantastical paradise where your senses will experience outlandish ecstasies. I am more perverse than ever, and I am aware of impossible desires mounting inside me. I want to bind you to my body with fiery kisses to consume your ardour and your will, and to empty your last drop of blood. I shall leave you only when you are a puppet with no strings, with no mind of your own. But then I shall be nothing but an empty, lifeless doll myself, for we shall both have spent our entire youth satisfying our vices and our passions. I love you, I do love you. Oh, that is the only thing I can think to say to you, for it alone encapsulates all the ardour, all the fire of my young senses, and I also know that you love me.

Tomorrow we shall witness this ardent love we have for each other. We can gauge the full extent of our madness, for we truly are mad, darling Charles, mad about each other. I now cannot think of you without shuddering from head to foot with urgent desire, and I cannot wait to give myself to you with all my might.

Oh, give me your arse which I adore, give me all the treasures of your voluptuous body, and take me, take all of me in demonic couplings, and empty me of everything down to the very marrow in my bones.

We shall love each other furiously tomorrow, in anticipation of still better things to come.

Do reply with a long letter so that when I see you tomorrow I can spill my come wildly into your mouth and over your cock.

I adore you, do you know that?

Simone

Sunday evening

This letter will not be very different from the others, from all the others, my adored one, and yet I know you are waiting for it with the same impatience as when you received my first note. That was nearly eighteen months ago. True to my promise, I shall send it first thing tomorrow so your anticipation is not disappointed.

My dear love, I am filled with tenderness this evening and I have only one regret: I cannot rest my head in your lap and tell you all the thoughts rising up from my heart to my lips. I wish you were here this evening, how blissful it would be! We would be reunited in this magical setting, and this big bed where our love was first born would be too broad an expanse for the two of us. For I would be huddled close up to your heart as I told you the words that will only be committed to paper this evening. And it is the same love song that I offer up to you every time, wrapping you in its sweet harmonies, giddying your senses and lulling your heart. My words, those same words again, will offer the best of my heart to you once more.

I love you to distraction, my dear beloved. Every ounce of me now only lives thanks to your ardent caresses. My longing for your body constantly torments me, and in the terrifying loneliness of the night, I reach my arms towards you in vain, embracing only emptiness, always emptiness. When I am far from you, I feel panic and despair, and your presence alone can soothe the anguish in my heart. I am bound to your flesh by all the embraces you have shown me, and nothing will ever be strong enough to tear me away.

You are beautiful, my lover, and I am in love with your beauty. I love your supple vigorous body, your arms which wrap around me and hold me tight, and your powerful thighs which bear down on my rump. I love your voluptuous lips whose kisses burn my skin, and more than anything else I love the wonderful look in your gorgeous eyes. Oh, those eyes, how they have ruffled my heart from that very first look! Oh, the flame that burned in them when they met mine the first time we saw each other! I already loved your eyes before I knew you. But now I adore them, for I can see your love and your desire in them, and they have such a beautiful bright expression which, under the effects of my ardent attentions, gradually darkens and goes out entirely when you climax. Yes, you are beautiful, Charles, and I am proud of you. And I love you more every day. In just a few days I shall be reunited with your wonderful body. Filled with boundless happiness, I shall smother it with kisses before taking it in a fierce embrace, for I am not sure how long I shall be able to resist my longing to bugger you forcefully, my darling little Lottie. It is many weeks now since you have surrendered your arse to me so I can probe it with my triumphant prick, and I want to repeat that brazen coupling for which you once hungered. And I know you are haunted by thoughts of it too, for I have before me the suggestive drawing from Arles. It is not me, you say, but what does that matter to me, for I am not far away, just a few paces from you? I am lying on my back with my thighs spread and a very young woman, almost a child, is sucking my cunt. And you are watching while your 'lover' drives his enormous prick into your hole. And, mutually aroused by these 'accomplices', we climax deliriously.

That is what you wanted to do, isn't it, darling? We would both be fulfilling an outrageous longing; the thought of it has dogged us relentlessly. But afterwards we would need no one more. It would be just the two of us, and we shall love each other. Yes, my loved one, I shall have the strength to overcome my secret resistance, and I shall hand you over to this lover you dream of having. And I too shall give myself to my mistress for you to see, and then you will know how much I love you, but we must be patient for I cannot really see how we could attempt this adventure before the summer.

Will you be satisfied by me alone until then? You know how ardently I am driven to give you pleasure, my beloved. Nothing can stop me and very soon, I should think, I shall prove that I am 'dirtier' than ever. You will wantonly surrender your beautiful body to me, and I shall sow kisses from your breasts to your balls, from your lips to your cock. My tireless tongue will lick and delve into the folds of your arse to prepare the way for the stiff tip of my big teat. Do you know anything more exciting than having your cock and your arse licked at the same time while your balls are stroked by a nimble hand? Yes, I want to try to make you come like that. Shall I succeed? I cannot be sure but it will give you a tremendous sensation and a powerful erection. There, I am spreading my thighs nice and wide, and putting my legs on your shoulders while my arms grip you around the waist. You can feel it go in right up to your balls. I sprinkle it constantly with an abundant flow of come, and my flesh contracts furiously around your dick. I keep spraying like the beautiful bitch that I am, again and again. Oh, you make me come, you filthy darling. Yes, fuck me again and forever, I love it.

On Friday perhaps, but definitely on Saturday, we shall be reunited in our room and we shall be free to indulge in our favourite exploits. I shall love you with unstinting ardour. Will you let me bugger you once more, even if only once? I shall be sensible and shall avoid jerking movements but I want you to be my little Lottie again, for I am afraid you are wearying of our embraces. Bugger me. Oh, darling, we really are filthy, the pair of us! Where are we going and whatever will next summer be like when we shall be free? Will we watch scenes of debauchery together as spectators, or shall we be the performers in scenes of our own? Whichever it is, we shall be happy, don't you think, Charles?

I love you, darling love, and I shall prove it to you once again when next we meet. And you, do you love me as much? On Friday you said, 'You know very well there is *only one* woman I love.' Is it me or the other woman? Tell me soon. Tell me you are deliriously happy in my arms, and that I alone fulfil all your desires and obligingly comply with *all your whims*, and that you will always keep me for yourself. Tell me quickly that you adore me. You have never told me whether I am the one *whom you prefer* in the lovemaking game. Which of us knows best how to make you come, her or me? Tell me at least once, my love. I adore you, Charles, Lottie. Till Tuesday, until there is anything better. Sending you frantic kisses, my dear love, wherever you want them.

Simone

I shall certainly feel some regret, my love, as I watch this wonderful year come to an end later this evening. Surely it has spoiled me terribly, for I have lived so many days with a heart full of happiness, and all my senses appeased by your tenderness and your caresses.

And as for this new year about to begin, you know that my dearest wish is to be in your arms as often as possible. Let's hope that, instead of separating us, this year will bring us together more, my loved one, and will bring us both the fulfilment we seek.

I hope your desires will finally be realised, my dear love, and that on some wild night we shall watch magnificent sights: women licking each other's arses, men sucking each other's cocks, and couples bound to each other in the lewdest embraces. And I hope you will finally find the vigorous man who will bring you to a devastating climax. Oh, I know how much pleasure it will give you to suck his huge cock. Your greedy, skilful mouth takes in every inch of it and you fondle his balls to give him an even bigger erection. You come, you filthy boy, but imagine the intoxication next when he buggers you right up to the hilt and now it is my mouth sucking on your cock.

Yes, this new year will probably see our wildest desires come true. I ask nothing but your love, as ever, and your touch on me. You are my little god, and I adore you. Look at me with your gorgeous big eyes, and take all of me in an endless embrace. Fuck me, fuck me, drive your huge cock into my cunt.

I love you.

Simone

1930

1930

Thursday morning

My dear treasure,
        However powerful my longing to write to you
yesterday evening, I was not at my leisure to do so, for I
had to host some unexpected guests.

Oh, but how I thought of you all evening, my love! I
had hardly left you and already I could feel my wild
craving for you rising again. I thought of the precious
minutes I have with you every evening, of the outrageous
things I say to you and the instant effect they have on
your cock. My, your beautiful prick does stand to attention quickly when I get onto particular subjects which
you and I hold dear! From the very first words, he fills
his pink head and then his entire body. He stands rigid,
magnificent, inside your trousers, and my hand can feel
him, can make him out, so hard and ready to ejaculate.
It would take only the subtlest bit more pressure, a slightly
longer stroking for a stream of come to be released from
your well-filled balls. This fondling in the complicit darkness of the street makes me long all the more for the time
together we have promised each other, and I arrive home
with my mind inflamed and my blood seething. Oh, how
I still love you, darling Charles, despite the months

219

marching by and all the extravagances we have already committed! My appetite for your attentions is still not sated. I crave them more and more. I require them, I want them and I am already dreaming of the supreme happiness afforded by our fierce couplings.

Tomorrow I shall probably be yours and you will be mine. I have now been waiting days on end for this wonderful time, waiting with the same fevered excitement, the same longing as before, in the early days of our love. But we were very well behaved then, my loved one, do you remember? We barely risked the occasional emboldened move, but now what is there that we would not dare do? We have tasted all the wildest pleasures and dreamed up the filthiest ministrations, and how happy it makes us, my darling treasure!

So tomorrow I shall be waiting for you in our little room. I shall undress and lie quite naked in the big bed, with the curtains drawn. You will barely be able to see me in the half-light, and your eyes will seek out your little mistress's rump, her breasts and her stomach. Your cock is already straining inside your trousers. He is pulsating. Oh really, come quickly, my beloved, come quickly.

And now you are beside me, also naked, and your flesh burns with the tide of desire washing over you. Give me your mouth, my darling. Give me your lips. Intoxicate me with your furious kisses. Ah, I am on top of you, can you feel me? I have gripped my thighs around yours, and pressed my groin against your cock which is rigid with insatiable desire. Oh yes, drive him in there, drive into my cunt. Make me come again, again and forever.

I want to teach you something tomorrow. I want to show you how to suck a dick. I shall put the 'substitute' between my thighs and you can take it in your mouth. While you stroke my curly hair above the ramrod, I will talk you through the moves, arousing you with my voice, and you will see how wonderful it is, my dear love. Of course, as you said yesterday, it cannot 'pay off'. That is true, and I wish I could offer you a real cock, a nice, big, hard living one. Oh yes, if we could have an accomplice, what a wonderful time we would have! Because I would be frantically aroused watching you grappling with him. I should like to watch you sucking a real prick. This is how I picture the scene: you are both on the bed, he at the foot and you at the head, and you are sucking at each other. I give you encouragement: 'Go on, go on, suck him, suck him, more, more. Suck my little Lottie well and you, my Lottie, you do the same for him.' The sight of your interlocked bodies drives me wild and I rub my button to intensify my own pleasure and yours. But enough. I want to be an accomplice in your games too. I lie on my back and you start fucking me, and at the same time he buggers you. You reach a double climax because you have the pleasure of being in my cunt and you can feel his great prick in your arse.

It would be wild to taste such pleasures, don't you think, my beloved? Are we really perverted enough? Let's hope that, some day, we can realise this outlandish dream.

Oh, I love you, my dear treasure. I love you more and more. I cannot cope without you now. I want to keep you forever. *You are my only love*, my only beloved, and without you love holds no appeal for me. You are the fairy-tale lover who has conquered my flesh and whose skilled ministrations kindle my desire. Beloved darling, do you still love me as much despite the passage of time? Do you still long for my body just as ardently? Do you long to experience another woman's touch? Oh, I am so afraid of losing you that I wish I were the person-ification of vice to bind you to me forever. Don't ask another woman for these exhausting kisses, don't surrender your cock to other lips than mine, and keep your arse for me, keep it for me alone so I can bugger it with fierce passion.

I should like to have a long letter from you this evening. I shall reply to it, and tomorrow we can read my answer together. Would you like that, darling love? Please go to the trouble and hurry and write me one of those adorable letters like the ones you write when we are apart.

Goodbye, my darling treasure, till this evening, but more importantly till tomorrow. Oh, how I shall love you!

Simone

Thursday, 5.30 p.m.

My darling love,
       You will read this letter in my arms. I shall not
send it this evening, for I want to test the power I have
over your senses, and witness your body's arousal when
you decipher these passionate words tomorrow.

Tomorrow is nearly upon us, with all its usual attendant
voluptuous delights, joys and sadistic couplings, and I
shall prove filthier than ever, as dirty a bitch as you could
wish for, to make your prick good and hard, and fill your
balls with generous come for you to offload . . . where?
In my mouth, in my cunt, over my face? Who knows?
Who can second-guess the final moment which will
crown this festival of our senses?

Whatever happens, you can rest assured I shall put to
good use everything at my disposal to make you come
passionately.

We shall be alone again tomorrow. No 'accomplice'
will be there to participate, be it a vigorous male or the
delicate mistress of our dreams. We shall be alone and
yet not, not entirely, for they will in fact be there, these
accomplices of ours. Do we not both have a very clear
picture in our minds of the scenes we could act out

together? And I can tell that tomorrow they will be there to titillate our senses and make us behave all the more sadistically. He with his impressive cock straining with insatiable desire, and she circling my quivering button with her pink tongue.

Yes, the lover I have found for you is beautiful. His supple muscular body will very ably wrap its long firm thighs around you. His cock is beautiful too, with an imposing girth, and your pearly-white skin will stand out beautifully against his darker skin. I can picture the lewd tableau the two of you will make. His blond hair next to your brown hair, his smooth stomach against your arched arse, and your cock rearing between his vigorous hands. Yes, I would find it extraordinarily exciting to watch him pleasuring you, and even if you felt like buggering him in front of me, well, oh God, I would say very little for I should be pleasuring myself in front of you. But I admit I would rather feel your cock up my arse.

What about you, can you picture the scene? My mistress is on the bed, her little breasts pointing their pink nipples towards my mouth; I take them firmly. I lick them with quick little flicks of the tongue while sliding a hand between her thighs and frigging her. Meanwhile you are licking my arse. Then all at once my mouth travels down and presses itself to her quivering button. Watch me eating her arse, the little pig. Give her your cock, she can tug you while I watch. Now it is my turn to savour her lascivious attentions. She's sucking me, watch. Oh, she's so good at it, darling! Look how her tongue works lovingly at my flesh. Suck her too, go on, you have my permission. Make her come before my eyes. Slide your tongue into her cunt. It will make her attentions to me all the more frenzied. But go no further than that. Your cock is for me, for me alone. Come and fuck me now, come quickly. I shall release my sap all over your stiff ramrod. Take me in a never-ending coupling to make me surrender all of me.

I am not afraid, I am no longer afraid of passing time, for I now know what your passions are, and how to keep you by my side. And this summer I have every intention of letting you beat me, for I know that is your wildest dream, to whip my insolent rump till it bleeds and then to take me when I am still panting and broken.

Tomorrow, tomorrow, my dear love. I shall have your magnificent body, and I shall feel your adorable lips caressing my burning flesh. In the meantime, I can but spend the whole night with a heart brimful of ardent longing for every ounce of your body, my dear lover whom I adore.

I hope you will be truly filthy to rival your darling dirty bitch. Tell me things to excite my audacious imagination. Make my button swell with your filthiness, and you just watch how ardently I shall love you.

Goodbye, my darling little love, till tomorrow. While you read this letter, I shall suck your cock or your little pink breasts, and I shall watch the feral glint of desire develop in your eyes, making you throw yourself onto the bed with your legs apart and your prick standing to attention. Then I shall straddle you and it will drive into my cunt right up to your balls.

I adore you, my dirty little darling.

Simone

Thursday, midnight

I cannot sleep, my Charles, I am appallingly unhappy and my heart feels heavy. I find myself wondering what has happened to you; all of a sudden you have grown so indifferent, so detached from our love that you have managed to go three long weeks, nearly a month, without seeing me alone.

I promise you I cannot believe you have had enough of me, for I know you well and I know that, before, you would not have been able to resist the need to savour all our embraces, to be given proof of my love, to surrender at last to one of the wild climaxes which formed the basis of our complicity. It now feels as if none of this tempts you any more. If I ask when I can see you, you tell me you are the only person manning the office or you cannot make up your mind, or lord knows what else.

I beg you, Charles, stop inflicting this suffering on me. Dispel the misunderstanding between us with a word. Tell me your answer and tell me soon, whatever it may be. This evening we parted almost angrily. You gave me no answer. You left me in such a hurry and now here I am wondering what is wrong.

I do not resent you for this, my treasure, you know that, but try to understand me. Remember our past together. Remember when we both burned with the same feverish longing to see each other. We threw ourselves on each other in an ever-increasing frenzy, and our two bodies would soon be convulsing to the same spasms. Can it be that none of this has any appeal for you now, and am I no longer your filthy darling who could make you come so wonderfully with my daring attentions?

Charles, my darling, if your desire for me has died, be loyal and do not drag my pain out any longer. Tell me it is all over and I shall know there is nothing more I can try to win you back. But for pity's sake, my love, spare me this protracted agony.

Charles, my little Lottie, I am very sad because I really think I am alone in cherishing our wonderful past. So, tell me, do you no longer want me, does my arse no longer tempt you with the silky skin of my buttocks, and has my mouth lost its incredible powers which once made your cock stiffen between its lips? But why did my tongue feel him so gorgeous and big yesterday evening if you are never to drive him into me again? Oh, my treasure, my treasure, can you really have grown so indifferent? And I still want you so desperately. I am in pain, my darling, and you do not want to understand. Why did you not answer my questions yesterday evening? Why did you leave so quickly? But I implore you, my adored one, take pity on my suffering. Tell me what is wrong. Why are you spurning me? It cannot possibly be that you have not found just one hour in the last three weeks to spend in my arms.

I am not angry, my love. If you could see me now, you would pity me. I am lying quite naked in my rumpled bed and I am weeping, my Charles, I am weeping, for I have such a strong feeling that you are breaking away from me.

Oh, darling, this is not the letter I was dreaming of sending you from this bed, but will it have any sort of allure for you now?

My darling love, must I give up all our pleasures? Must I drive all memories of your magnificent body from my mind, and will my own body never feel your arms around it again? Oh, my adored Charles, I must be wrong, I am wrong, surely? You still love me, you have not wearied of my big arse or my breasts, or my entire body which bent to your whims. Picture my buttocks reaching brazenly towards your cock. Think back to that little brown hole you once loved so much. And think of my tongue caressing your buttocks and your balls, and sliding the full length of your prick from head to root. Close your eyes and think of him here in my mouth, and your life flowing drop by drop into my throat. Then you will have a clearer idea of whether it is over between us, because if none of these memories make you tighten your fingers around your ramrod, then I have lost my power and, sadly, I was right.

My Charles, are you still my little Lottie, my delicious little mistress, the woman for whom I wanted to find a vigorous male, or do you now want to discover such pleasures alone?

I do not believe you have any doubts about my faithfulness, or that you feel this watch I now wear is a sign that I have lapsed. No, my love. He is like all the others, he has only ever had vague hopes about me, and he left without knowing my mouth's sweet caress which he so longed to savour you know where. Had I been able to do it in front of you, perhaps I would have made him very happy but, alas, my adored Charles, you know I do not even have the strength or the will to betray you. You have imprisoned my heart and my senses far too securely. I am yours, only yours, for all time.[21]

Goodbye, treasure, I shall try to sleep. I beg you one last time, answer me, even if your reply causes me the greatest heartache of my life. I would prefer anything to your silence and this torture.

---

21 Now that Simone has accepted and integrated the idea of another male partner into their relationship, she becomes obsessed with it and by doing so demonstrates further her hysteria, although this does not make her a nymphomaniac. No part of this story suggests that she had any affairs with another man over the course of her romance with Charles, and, in spite of her excesses, I believe she was sincere and loyal.

Come, my darling, let me kiss the wonderful body you are denying me.

Your filthy little darling is suffering so much without you, my loved one. Answer me, I beg of you. Till Monday???

Simone

The absence of Charles's letters does nothing to hinder our reading or our understanding of the relationship, because Simone's neurotic verbal outpourings, which seem to lead the way in this game of pleasures and desires, keep us abreast of developments. There are times, however, when a letter from Charles would help us to see him as a three-dimensional person. Through the prism of Simone's missives, it becomes clear that her lover has a sense of weariness (or panic?) after each new pleasure, and we start to suspect that as he follows the trajectory of his 'depravity', his progress feels like that of a pilgrim on the way to Santiago de Compostela: he takes two steps back for every three steps forward. If they had been found Charles's letters might have given us useful insights into how he was feeling at this point, but we can infer that the urge to explore his illicit desires further was tempered with a haunting sense that to fulfil them would mean doing something irreparable. Which is why the spectre of separation is ever-present. It is easier for Charles to resent Simone rather than himself for this journey along the forbidden pathways of his temptations. At what point, then, would his desires lose the upper hand over his fear of moral bankruptcy?

It is highly likely that these letters to Charles could only have been found in what had once been Simone's own cellar, and not her lover's. As well as this correspondence, the leather satchel also contained letters from a previous relationship, and many more relating to other minor affairs of Simone's, right back to her adolescence. But if they were sent to other people, how, you might think, would they have been found in her possession and not in that of each relevant man? There is a simple explan- ation, one that relates to a widely observed code of honour in love affairs in France (and well catalogued in eight- eenth- and nineteenth-century French literature): in polite society, custom dictated that when lovers broke up, the man should return all the letters that had been sent to him, so there could be no risk of compromising the lady's reputation later. This is a far cry from today's morality when so many aggrieved lovers post intimate 'revenge porn' images on Facebook, and the shameless partners of public figures show no restraint in their media- circus confessions.

We are very lucky that Simone didn't destroy the letters Charles returned to her (and, incidentally, she would probably also have returned his letters to him but it would be miraculous if these were ever found); there seems little doubt that Simone continued to view this relationship as extraordinary for the rest of her life, and therefore couldn't bring herself to dispose of them. For Charles, as a married man, the page had to be turned and the pages of this affair destroyed.

My tender love,
     Your *pneu* has come and soothed all my fears. Although very short, it was enough to see happiness blossom once more in the ardent bosom of your half-crazed mistress who is so quick to despair. And this evening I am sitting at my little writing desk perusing the hasty sketch of your triumphant cock. He is here before my eyes as I write these words, and he almost seems to be coming to life.

     Yes, my tender sweetheart, that is how I like to see that bold and beautiful prick, and I wish I could take all of it into my mouth, suck on it expertly, trailing my agile tongue over its smooth warm skin, and feeling its bitter come which I so love deep in my throat. Yes, I remember: the deserted street, the two of us, all alone. Quickly, give me your cock, Charles darling, it's already hard. A dab of my tongue was all it took and there, out in the street, with horrifying audacity, we risked that ultimate exploit. I sucked you. Ah, nothing can stop us, my loved one, nothing. Don't you pleasure yourself almost every evening while I describe a thousand wild excesses for you, to fuel your ardour? You can hardly be surprised then, my treasure, that I should complain about this fast you are imposing on me, for you must surely suspect that, being so close to you and touching you with my tongue and hands, I can barely go on living. Just think, three interminable weeks have passed since last we were together. A three-week trip to Bandol, and I want you, I want you so much I could scream, so furious and acute is my desire for every inch of your body, every ounce of your flesh. Yes, my treasure, I want you quite naked in my arms, I want the soft caress of your skin stroking against mine. My powerful thighs imprison yours, and I can feel your cock against my stomach, stiffening with helpless longing. There, look, I'm giving you my cunt as a haven, your beautiful much loved cock. Drive your proud head into that soft inviting nest. Each thrust of my hips forces you deeper inside. There, there, again, again. Ah, how adorable and unimaginable it is coming like that. Yes, fuck me, screw me, you darling bastard, I cannot wait a moment longer. Oh, darling, when can we go back to our discreet room which has witnessed our most magnificent battles? I shall be as filthy as you like, my loved one. I want you to spend the most incredible moments in my arms. Will you want to thrust that beautiful ramrod up me? I am sure you remember it, my treasure. I was being buggered and fucked at the same time, and through the thin wall of my cunt you rubbed your prick against the 'other man', and you were happy,

235

my love. I cannot wait to see my Lottie's glorious arse, and her little brown hole ready to submit to a vigorous male's staggering assaults. Don't forget, my darling, I want to be the one who guides this long-dreamed-of prick towards your arse with my hands. In the meantime, you know I have a spectacular toy between my thighs to prepare the way. But my mouth and tongue alone will be up to the task, for I so crave that adorable little brown hole that I feel sure I would happily do without the 'stand-in'. Oh, darling, the day you are finally free and call me to you, you will surrender your body to a more frenzied mistress than ever. Oh, darling, I can bear it no longer. I want you desperately. Yes, it feels as if you have gone a long way away and will soon be back. Remember our lovemaking when you return from your travels, darling treasure. How furiously we give ourselves to each other! I have faith in you, my loved one. Forgive me if I doubted your tender feelings, but also remember you have not schooled me to cope with such a long wait except when you are travelling. Did I have a right to panic, my sweet darling? So then, I shall wait. I shall master my impatience, but when you are in my arms again, oh, darling, what new follies we shall commit! I really am quite a bitch, wouldn't you say? We shall go back out into the deserted street if you still cannot come to me this week. I adore you, treasure, and I am waiting for you more lovingly than ever.

I am nestling in your arms with my head in the crook of your shoulder and my thighs over your stomach, and I am slowly kissing your mouth and your eyes which I adore.

Till Monday evening, darling.

Simone

My dearly loved darling,
 True to my promise, before going to bed I have come to write this letter you are expecting, this letter which you did not find when you reached Narbonne and which was the cause of the horrors that almost happened to us.

My loved one, I am profoundly happy to have been reunited with you. Yesterday I thought it was all over. Forgive me once again, oh, my dear darling.

You know very well I love you more than anything in the world. I am yours from the very depths of my being and of my heart, and when I think of all our embraces, I can feel myself dying just as I die beneath your kisses. Ah, how wonderfully well you took me, my love, and how wonderfully well you have learned to keep hold of me, for I have not stopped loving you for a moment from the first day. In a few days' time, we shall have reached our second anniversary, my beloved. Cast an eye back and see how high we have climbed. Remember our first quick shy fondling and think of how we spend our time together now. More importantly, think of the times we shall have in the future when we are both freed of the chains that bind us and can escape for a whole night to the wonderful paradise conjured and exhorted by our longing.

Yes, Charles, the time will soon come when you can at last experience the ultimate sensual pleasure. First of all, if you want it, we shall have the prelude to this debauchery here, in my house. The big bed will play host to three bodies, three naked forms in the shaded light, affording glimpses of thighs and arms and heads, a great accumulation of warm pink flesh, and your voluptuous moans will soar through the darkness. You will watch your mistress, your big dirty bitch, sucking wildly at her young, dark-pelted girlfriend. She will hold her mysterious little button between her lips and feel it swell to her kiss, while her agile hands wander over the girl's quivering body. Watch her, just watch that young virgin climax to her mistress's kisses . . . see how her stomach shudders, see how her breasts swell . . . She gasps and cries as these expert ministrations make her swoon . . . You can hold out no longer, you push her aside violently and now it is your turn to suck your mistress. Your cock is hard and full of come, so tempting for my mouth . . . Come here, I want you to swoon to my kisses too. Give me that big prick . . . Ah! There, there, feel my tongue running the full length of its smooth, warm skin . . . My tongue goes up, and up again . . . towards the head, then back down all the way to the balls . . . yes, you want to offload in my mouth, you dirty boy, I can tell . . . You can bear it no longer . . . Go on, push it right down my throat, give all of it to me, all of it down to the last drop. Then, to rekindle your desire, I ask my girlfriend to frig me and suck me in front of you. Our bodies adopt the most brazen positions. Now you see her arse, now mine and you have a furious erection again. So, while she pleasures herself, you and I make love in front of her, and you fuck me, my love, you make me come till I beg for mercy.

A bedroom there; together we have chosen a fine young boy with a generous body, a beautiful cock and a beautiful arse. You are lying naked on the bed and your lover is ready to satisfy you. He lies down beside you and soon his hand is tugging your cock, but his is not hardening fast enough for my liking. Here, let me help him; I take his member in my mouth while he masturbates you. Watch your mistress down between his legs. She is kneeling and you can reach out a hand and stroke her big arse, but his shaft is perfectly stiff now . . . Come on, Lottie, kneel by the side of the bed. Your hole is already half open, so tormented are you with longing. A thrust of your lover's hips, and you gasp, touched to your very depths. His big balls bash against your arse while his cock plunges into your hole. My Charles, you are being buggered by a real cock, and you will soon feel his warm come drenching you. To heighten your pleasure, I take your cock between my lips, and you come in my mouth like the beautiful bitch that you are. Meanwhile, I frig myself vigorously, drunk on the sight of this tableau, and the three of us roll around pell-mell, smothered in come and exhausted by our shared climax.

Is that really what you want, my love? Is that the last sensation I must give you? Oh, how happy I shall be that day, my Lottie . . .

Tell me you want to continue our dream together just as much as I do. Tell me you still need to feel my body on yours. But also tell me that you still love me, despite the passing time, despite our little disagreements, in spite of everything!

As for me, Charles, I adore you. You know I shall never turn away. You do not always understand me, and this sometimes hurts me. Do let's stop tearing each other apart, my love, it is too painful. Let's love each other as we did before, let's love each other with the fire we once had, and if we can, let's add more wonderfully passionate and depraved moments to our memories. We should go together to find the beautiful bastard who will fulfil all our last desires, would you like that, Lottie?

You will receive this letter tomorrow just as you wanted. It is very late, I shall stop writing. I too should like to have a few pages from you in reply to this letter, to draw the last pictures hovering around my happiness. Will you do that, darling? You know how I love your letters; they are so rare, they have become so rare. Make me happy, darling treasure, make a little effort and on Friday I shall have a delicious letter which will make my button swell helplessly.

Goodbye, my dear darling treasure, I shall go to sleep thinking of you. I love you with all my soul, do you know that, my Charles? And I want to keep you forever and ever.

Write soon to tell me you love me too.

Pressing myself against you, treasure. I adore you.

Your Simone

M y great love,
       True to the promise I made yesterday, I am
sending the letter you requested. And yet what can I tell
you that you have not already known for a long time, my
beloved? Did my last letter not describe once again all
our most ardent, our most secret desires, and do you not
now know all the follies we shall soon commit?

You want me yet again to give you a long-distance
erection, my beautiful filthy darling, and you will most
likely be alone when your read these words at your office,
sitting with your thighs spread and your cock in your
hand. I can picture the scene as I write, and I wish I were
there now to watch it first-hand.

Whatever will it be like then, my love, when you watch
me take my little girlfriend in my arms and we ride each
other on the bed in a fiery embrace? Whatever will it be
like when I suck a gorgeous big prick in front of your
eyes?

Yes, my darling love, we shall commit a thousand follies
when we have one or two beautiful accomplices. I shall
invent obscure pleasures to make every ounce of you
quiver. When the two of you are really good and hard, I

shall rub your two pricks together. I shall bring your two bulging pink heads together. It must be an exquisite sensation, touching another man's cock with your cock. Don't you think, darling beloved? If I only could, I should like my mouth to be big enough to suck you both at the same time, but what I want to see is you and your 'lover' sucking each other's cocks in an impressive '69'.[22] Meanwhile, the two of us, the other two players, will be usefully occupied, for we shall be doing the same, and the four of us shall then form two intermingled couples in a scene of indescribable debauchery. If you do not have faith in this man's ability to suck you, then I shall do it and he, meanwhile, can bugger you with all his might, right up to his balls. Last time we met I gave you a foretaste of that rare coupling, and you seemed to find it deliciously pleasurable. We shall do it again sometime soon if you would like, my love. Then you will be able to wait more patiently for the great day itself.

You know I am prepared to try every adventure with you, whatever it might be. No action, no idea to please you would meet with my resistance, for what I want above anything else is for you to have such powerful experiences in my arms that you would not think of

---

22 Readers may be surprised to see the term '69' being used here; however, after some Internet research I found its first usage in a quote dating back to 1893 (although with no author reference given).

leaving me to seek them elsewhere. I show no hesitation in throwing you between the thighs of a handsome man, but, oh, what if you prefer him to me? I know the pleasure you will have, my love, when you feel that wonderfully hard rod of flesh up your arse, delving every angle of your most secret folds. You will feel that huge head slowly stroking the furthest walls of your insides, for the sensation is so powerful it is as if you are being probed right inside your stomach. It is hallucinatory and exquisite. It is maddeningly arousing and wonderful, and you yourself can have only a meagre notion of the pleasure afforded by a cock offloading in your arse. At this very moment, that cock is swelling and swelling, and you can feel that warm stream showering over you. Oh, I run every risk of losing you by giving you this passionate experience, for will you make do with the feeble means at my disposal once you have come like that? This will be the greatest proof of love I have ever given you, for with it I risk all my happiness.

For it is this that you are asking me to show you, my little Lottie, am I right? You will be satisfied, I know you will, unless you back down at the last moment. But no, you are a gorgeous filthy bastard and all your dreams are filled with pricks and balls. When you are in my arms, you think of this lover, the lover I must give you, and you thrill in anticipation with barely contained desire.

If you want, we shall spend many a wonderful hour together this summer. We can have a few moments together every evening before having to part, or you could come and join me in my 'bachelor flat'. We can spend an hour together, making love at our leisure and committing a thousand follies. Would you like that, my beloved? I shall invite my little girlfriend and the three of us can perform every possible filthy exploit. If we manage to find a 'bastard', we can invite him too.

My love, we are bound by our all-powerful debauchery which chains us to each other, to bring us endless happiness. Can you even imagine lovemaking now without all these exalted but perverse ministrations? Can you imagine loving a quiet, prudish mistress? I for one could not make love with another lover but you; the very thought of belonging to another man makes me smile. You once told me: 'It's not as if you don't want to.' Don't go thinking that, darling Lottie, for I love you alone, you can be sure of that. If others hope to charm me, do they have your beautiful bottomless eyes, or your hot tender lips which are so good at kissing my mouth? More particularly, do they have that wonderful body, or that warm silky skin on which I like to rest my cheek? And that beautiful, big hard cock which works such wonders between my thighs?

My darling little treasure, my little god, how I love you and how happy I am! I hope I shall prove it to you soon, for I want you very much, my beloved. And what about you? Do you not want to fondle my body? Do you not want to press your ardent kisses onto this arse you once adored? Think of all the fantastical ecstasies you owe to that lovely big firm white backside, but how you abandon it now! You want my mouth, only my mouth, to give you an erection, to make you come, to suck you, you big filthy darling.

No point telling you I am now going to bed and, oh, how terribly all these excesses have aroused me! I shall lie down naked on the fur cover on my bed and, thighs spread and stomach taut, I shall frig myself vigorously while I think of everything you would do to me if you were beside me.

Goodbye, my dear love. I hope you will receive this letter on Monday. Telephone me soon to tell me whether you like it and whether you have time. Write me a long reply on Tuesday.

Till Monday, darling treasure. I adore you.

Your Simone

My dear treasure,

I have been very sad all day, for the letter I was expecting this morning never arrived. But I have been rewarded this evening, for I have it in my hands at last, and I have never read one better designed to excite my senses. My letters may please you, my love, but what can I say of yours?! They put me in the wildest of states. So I have just reread at my leisure the four pages you handed me, and my button is as stiff as your cock would be before a titillating performance. I see so much of you in it, my darling little bastard. Yes, you are a beautiful debauched creature, and I love you all the more for it, for you afford me moments of intense voluptuous delight.

One evening when you are free, as I am, we shall savour the wild exhilaration which obsesses us both. Come, I very much want to find a companion-in-vice for each of us, one to bugger you just the way you want, a beautiful, vigorous well-endowed male, whose cock you can suck and whose balls you can fondle, and who will rub your dick with a frenetic hand. Subjected to his brutal attentions, you will feel your strength drain away, you will cry out with both pain and pleasure. Do you picture the scene as I do? You are lying on your side. Your 'man' is buggering you. I kneel in front of you and suck you while the other accomplice fucks me. What I should also like would be to be fucked while at the same time vigorously pleasuring two cocks. Oh, I am not sure what I want now, you are making me lose my mind. Yes, perhaps I would agree to your fucking another person in front of me. I would watch your cock disappearing into my girlfriend's cunt, while I frigged myself. But I should like you to see me sucking her with my deft tongue to pump out her come. I feel sure you would be rigid with insatiable desire at the sight of such a scene. And then you in turn would offer up your member for my ardent attentions. My loved one, I am happy you have such arousing sensations in my arms, and nothing gives me greater pleasure than sucking your lovely cock after it has made me come so wonderfully. When it comes out of me, it is so hard that it feels ready to burst with the pressure of the come inside it, and emptying it is an incomparable pleasure for me. Yes, I put all my skill into this act, for I adore it. Sucking you is my favourite thing. My button is swelling just at the thought of it.

We shall soon enjoy the debaucheries we have promised ourselves, but in the meantime you will make me die with pleasure. I shall be more depraved, more passionate than ever, and I shall excite you with my perverted words and deeds.

Give me all of you. I am bringing my tender, tender lips to your beloved eyes.

Simone

My dear darling love,

I told you yesterday evening that we have found the partner to help us realise our ultimate dream, and I wonder whether I succeeded in satisfying you. I had a vague but painful feeling that some part of you was baulking at the idea that I had managed to come this far, that I had managed to ask this man to join us. I wonder, Charles darling, whether you are a little angry with me for being so bold, and I am very sad to think I may have displeased you.

You know how much I love you, my dear treasure, and how much I want you to find ever more happiness in my arms. You know the full extent of the tenderness I have shown for you for nearly two years, and I hope you also know that you are my one and only and true love. So, as I have a constant need to please you and a still more burning need to keep you for myself, I have put all my depravity in the service of my love. I have known for a long time that you wanted to experience the brutal, un-familiar attentions of a man as ardent and dirty as we are. I know you want to feel between your lips the beautiful soft skin of a nice long hard prick, and you are even more eager to feel it up your arse. I sought and I found. Are you angry with me, my beloved, for having gone almost halfway to achieving your satisfaction?

It is now entirely up to you, Lottie, if you want to experience this ultimate ecstasy. If you want it, you can soon surrender yourself to this man's embraces. Perhaps he will suck you more fiercely than I can, and you can reciprocate. You will hold his big cock between your lips while I suck on yours. Your hands can fondle his balls bursting with come, while I frig myself for you both to see. Would it not arouse you, then, to feel a real prick between your lips, to feel it swelling in your mouth, and also to put your own cock into a man's mouth? You will no longer have a fervent mistress between your thighs, but a vigorous male with an erection like a dirty bastard, for, to arouse him in preparation for this debauchery, you and I shall couple fiercely before his eyes, and he will be unable to resist such a scene. You will see his big cock straining helplessly towards your arse, and he will claim your hole, taking brutal possession of it as he drives his hard dick in up to the balls, and then you will have that supreme voluptuous sensation.

If you dare not be the one to touch him first, I shall do it for you, in front of you. I shall suck his cock while he tugs yours, and you can frig me too, at the same time. We shall be three gorgeous bastards, all quite naked, and our bodies will take each other on in strenuous, peculiarly indecent positions. You said in your last letter that you

251

would not be against watching me being taken by our partner. If you want, if it will help arouse you, I shall give myself to him while you watch. You can watch our every move. If the scene gives you new strength, you can follow straight after him and take me in a fierce coupling, fucking me furiously right up to your balls, for my pleasure will be complete only if I can be sure you are happy, my dear love. I do not doubt for one moment that you will derive the rarest of pleasures from these new games *but I shall do nothing without your formal consent.*

I know this man is a beautiful bastard like you and me, who stop at nothing and are afraid of nothing. He is a good strong lad who must surely have a well-hung cock. I felt it only through his trousers to reassure myself you would not be disappointed by its girth. But you seem to be holding this liberty against me, and that is what upsets me so. I shall tell you again, my darling love, it was for your sake that I showed such audacity. I wanted to keep my promise and give you the sensation you have wanted for such a long time, but if you do not feel you have the heart to see this adventure through to the end, *if, more importantly, you should withdraw your love* once I have given myself to this man *in front of you*, we must stop in our tracks and never attempt anything like this again.

If, on the other hand, you would step out of this house a happy man, if you have it in you to appreciate this ultimate proof of my love, then we must do it, and soon.

I shall expect your answer tomorrow evening, Charles. You must reply tomorrow. I shall do nothing without knowing what you want.

Would you rather give up the idea of this cock and these balls you could fondle to your heart's content? Or do you want me to throw you between that beautiful bastard's thighs? Ah, I should like to watch the two of you taking turns to suck each other. I should like to watch your slightly awkward manoeuvres as you tug each other at the same time. Did you not once write that you used to pleasure your little school friends? Well, you can repeat the performance in front of me. You will masturbate him with passionate gestures, and when his cock is nice and hard, you can put it in your mouth and you will feel his come pulsing right to the back of your throat in a powerful stream. Or I could be the one to suck him in front of you, and when his member is stiff and ready to come, I shall steer it towards your already opened hole, and he can come inside you.

And would you not like to bugger him too? How will you come, my love? Most likely in my mouth. I can picture a position you would find very arousing, I am sure of it. I am lying on my back with my legs apart. You put your arse on my face. I lick your arsehole and reach round to pleasure your cock with one hand. Meanwhile, facing you, right before your eyes, you can watch the other man driving his cock into me. Would it not be exhilarating to come like that, my darling treasure?

Think about it. You can give me a long letter tomorrow, telling me what you think of this partnership. I do not want to give an answer until I have yours. Imagine what the three of us could do. Think particularly about the fact that, with all three of us in a heightened sexual state, I shall not be able to escape this man's clutches, and you will have to watch me ravished in his arms. Will this not be galling for you, Charles, seeing me taking pleasure from another man's caresses? Will you still love me as much afterwards, my treasure?

Oh, do you know, I myself am now wondering whether I should accept this, for I am afraid of losing you, my beloved. You looked so astonished yesterday when I told you everything. Whatever will it be like when you see me in his arms?

And yet, my darling love, you know it is you alone I love, and I cannot love another lover but you. If I am prepared to try this, it is to give you still more unusual sensations. Do you want to experience them like this?

The other man has no effect on me, I told you that, I do not love him. It is you that I love, and I shall be in his arms only long enough for one coupling. Afterwards it is you that I want. Your chest, your neck, your arms. You will be my refuge, my love, and I shall come to rest, huddled against you.

Oh, my darling Lottie, I would be giving you beautiful proof of my love by doing this. I shall have left no stone unturned to make you happy above all else. I would prostitute myself to give you a partner worthy of you. You must love me truly deeply, my treasure, as my reward.

I shall wait for your reply tomorrow evening. You must find the time to write to me, if only a single line to *tell me all your thoughts*, with absolutely no reservations. I should be very disappointed if you did not, my love.

Goodbye, my dear treasure whom I adore. When shall we next be together in our little room to love each other? How you have abandoned me recently, my darling!

I am furiously impatient to see you again tomorrow, my darling one.

How I love you, how I do love you! You are my whole life, my whole happiness. I am yours from the depths of my soul, and my body will remember your touch for the rest of my days. If only we could always belong to each other like this, oh, my wonderful darling whom I adore!

Passionate kisses on your lips and all over you, Charles, you whom I love more than anything in the world, my tender love.

Your Simone

Charles, it seems, is backing away from the temptation of a homosexual experience. Obviously, the social context of his time did not look favourably on such orientations. Although homosexuality had been decriminalised in France since a revolutionary decree in 1791, homophobia was still rife in most circles, including among many intellectuals, such as Paul Claudel who asserted his stance unequivocally. The publication of Gide's **Corydon** *in 1924 elicited violent diatribes, and vengeful libellous comments. ('La nature a horreur du Gide', which is a pun on the French expression for 'Nature abhors a vacuum', plays on the similarity between the French word for vacuum, 'vide', and the name of the homosexual author Gide, to give us 'Nature abhors a Gide'. An English equivalent, though lacking the elegant familiarity of an existing truism, might be 'It goes against nature to be so Wilde'.)*

Things were further complicated by the fact that the newly emerging field of psychiatry filed 'sexual inversion' alongside mental illness; this meant that the more liberal moral landscape, which is likely to have allowed many homosexuals considerable freedom to find fulfilment, and spared them the fear of criminal prosecution, still went hand in hand with widespread disapproval. This period of conditional freedom in France came to an

end under Pétain's regime with the adoption in 1942 of
a law which repressed all manifestations of homosexual
relations, and would have consequences far beyond the
end of the war: homosexuality was declared a scourge
on society in 1960, and was added to the list of mental
illnesses in 1968. It was not until 1982 that it was decrim-
inalised, and 1985 that it was withdrawn from the
Diagnostic and Statistical Manual of Mental Disorders.

My most adored love,
I am shaking all over as you are, filled with frenetic desire at the thought of the follies we shall soon commit.

I waited anxiously for your reply, my loved one, and should have been very sad had you not given it to me this evening. But I have it, I have your letter. I am clasping it to my heart, for in it I can hear a cry from deep inside you, a cry suffocated by the surge of violent desire coursing feverishly through your veins.

Oh, how I love you, my beautiful darling bastard, and how I shall enjoy watching you swoon to your partner's touch! Yes, I have found a beautiful, good big hard cock for you. I have felt it and squeezed it feverishly with my fingers and in my hand, I felt its hard head coming strangely to life. While I described your beautiful body in passionate terms, I could feel our partner growing wildly aroused and I was happy, my love, to know I could give him an erection like that just by talking of you, for I could already see all the pleasure I would soon be able to give you, my Lottie whom I adore.

Yes, adored darling, you really will have to love me now, for you will never doubt me again when I have kept this last promise.

You asked to know what our partner wants. All I can do is relay what he said: he wants to suck your cock, he wants to pleasure you with his hand, and he most likely would want you to do the same for him, I imagine. So you will have to take his prick between your lips and, remembering my lessons, make this male member stand rigidly to attention.

I shall help you, my love, for I suspect the three of us shall be a little embarrassed seeing each other quite naked like that, in these circumstances, and I shall come to the aid of whichever of you is the shyer. Above all, don't forget that what would truly drive him into a frenzy would be to watch us making love in front of him. We shall therefore provide him with a performance of our most demented couplings. You and I shall be utterly filthy, and he will be incapable to controlling himself for long.

I am dreaming of this supreme debauchery, my love. I can already picture our three bodies embroiled in one embrace, our thighs tangled with each other, our heads muddled together, and there, between the two of you, I shall arouse you as much as I can with my words and actions.

I shall tug you both at the same time. I shall take you in turns to suck your cocks. I shall submit my body to your wildest desires. And to reward me for such audacity, you will treat me to the rare sight of your brutal couplings. Oh, what a tableau, your two bodies squirming together, two cocks and two pairs of balls emerging from this mass of rutting flesh! I feel sure I shall not be able to resist the pleasure of frigging before your eyes, and the bolder of you two will come to gather the sap from my cunt.

In order to arouse you, I shall be the proud dirty bitch you love. I want to ensure our partner is hard so you can offer up your magnificent arse to be assailed by him. What a victory, my love, if he probes your hole with his huge member, if he buggers you right up to the hilt! I want you to feel his hot come deep inside you, flooding your innards, and I want to hear you groan with pleasure at this fierce embrace. When you have savoured every possible sensation in his arms, you can come and bestow your caresses on me. You can fuck my cunt with all the skill you bring to that coupling, you can suck my button swollen with come, you can tug yourself over my chest, and then you can come at last in my mouth.

Then, my love, I will have done everything I can to make you happy and to realise your ultimate wish. If it does not afford you the most complete pleasure, well then, we shall look elsewhere, but I think we shall not be disappointed.

There, my darling love, we shall be able to do all this, and soon, I hope, I shall tell you everything I know.

Then, over the course of this coming summer, I hope I can give you another pleasure, my love. I very much hope my young girlfriend will be in Paris at the same time as us, so we can spend an evening together here, in my home. You would have two women by your side, and you will see I can suck a cunt just as well as a cock, my love.

I hope the two of us shall also have some wonderful times alone together, for I truly love our private two-somes. After all this debauchery, I would like to return to our past pleasures and to love each other one-to-one. Our embraces have their own profound charm, my Lottie, but will they be enough for you now?

You are my darling lover, and all these pleasures will only make me love you more. I already know how beautiful your body is, my little Lottie, and how soft your skin. I am sure I will be still more besotted with you, for you are beautiful, my young god, and nothing can ever match the body I adore.

All the same, we have come a long way in our depravity in these two years. What is there left for us to try? Nothing more.

I shall stop, my darling love. I shall try to sleep, but I am very afraid I shall dream of nothing but pricks and balls and arses.

Till Monday, my dear treasure. Holding you lovingly to me.

My lips ardently on yours. Yours, all yours.

Simone

My dear darling treasure,
I have just arrived home and, as you requested, I am writing this little note which you will have tomorrow morning.

When you read it, only a few hours will lie between us and the unbridled debauchery which has consumed our thoughts for months and months. Tomorrow I shall give you the partner whom I had the audacity to find for you. Tomorrow you will be able to gaze on his naked body, to surrender to all the excesses dictated by your passion. You can be sure he will accept your attentions, and will reciprocate them with the same fire.

I spoke to him this evening. He agrees to everything. You can be two gorgeous bastards together. You can take each other on shamelessly, and I shall arouse your passions with what I say and do. He will suck your cock and pleasure you with his hand, and you will do the same for him. You can take his prick in your mouth and bring him to an erection with a few skilled licks of your tongue.

True, he did not disguise the fact that he is a novice in this field as you are yourself, and he is very much relying on me to ensure this first instance goes well. So

I shall devote myself to the task, and I shall be the one to make the first moves.

We watched a beautiful naked dancer this evening. His muscled white body arched before our eyes. Every inch of him thrilled, and we talked about tomorrow's exploits. It will not be a stranger swooning before us tomorrow, but you, my Lottie, it is you, you filthy little bitch, who will squirm to those ardent kisses.

There, I have kept my promise. Tomorrow, I shall see you grappling with a beautiful bastard. I want you to reach passionate climaxes in his arms. Will you prove depraved enough for this? Will you be intimidated? No, for I shall be there, I shall help you.

Remember that, in order to excite your friend, we need to let him watch our embraces. You can prove your love for me in front of him, and you can be really filthy. I am in no doubt it will be successful, for the three of us are all proud bastards who will not shy away from anything as they strive for ever greater pleasure.

So make sure you are ready to suck a big prick and stroke a beautiful pair of balls tomorrow. You will also have to surrender your cock to your partner's attentions, and I hope you will feel the effects of his huge member.

Goodbye, my dear treasure. I am very tired. Forgive this slightly disjointed letter, but tomorrow words will be replaced by acts, and I know you will not complain then.

All of me is yours.

Simone

My adored treasure,
   You will find this letter tomorrow morning. I so hope it will rekindle the ardent ecstasies you felt on Saturday between our partner's thighs.

I will now always remember those two wildly alluring sights: firstly, you, after a moment's embarrassment, suddenly grasping his stiff prick and sucking it with tireless ardour, sucking that living, pulsing member in your mouth. My love, you were so happy at last to taste the warm soft skin of a beautiful erect cock. You closed your eyes and every inch of you tensed with feverish excitement, as you sucked greedily on that hardened ramrod, and to arouse you further I drove two fingers into your arse and buggered you furiously. Eventually you brought our friend to his climax and he sprayed his flow of sperm in your mouth. You discovered the taste of sperm which you have dreamed of for so long. A beautiful bastard just like you came between your lips and you fell back, wilting from the effort.

Then it was his turn to give you the same bold pleasure. I can still see you with your legs well apart, presenting your beautiful hard cock to his lips. He knelt before you and slowly sucked you, his tongue travelling awkwardly from your balls to the head. Then his attentions became more focused, his tongue strokes faster, and your ramrod shuddered and filled while you groaned at the voluptuous delight of it. But very soon one last skimming movement had the better of you, and your sperm spurted out, and I was the one who took the creamy sap in my mouth, for our friend was taken by surprise and was still moving up your shaft.

And now you know the wonderful sensation of sucking a cock. You held it between your lips, you licked it and kissed it, and you yourself climaxed thanks to a man's ministrations. I do not remember you climaxing in the same way to mine. I feel you were never quite so ecstatic. My love, if I have ever succeeded in giving you such tremendous pleasure, that makes me deeply happy myself, but the experience is not over yet. I would have liked you to savour the same joy, not in your mouth but in your big arse. Let's do it again, shall we? This first time, I hope you were not disappointed and that you have delicious memories of your initiation. I should like to know what you thought of it, my love. Write me a long letter telling me everything, and give it to me tomorrow.

What more would you like now, my dear treasure? What do want of me now? Would you like us to have an experience with a woman? Tell me if this picture would arouse you, my love: two beautiful bitches disappearing between each other's thighs, and making each other come by licking each other's buttons? You know I am holding my young girlfriend in reserve, she would not be against that sort of scene. She even telephoned me to say that her beau has asked to be introduced to us when he comes home this winter. His dream is to have the wildest of groupings . . . Tell me what you want, my pretty darling, and I will bow to your command. I hope we will be able to enjoy our friend's company again and that this time he will bugger you vigorously. He has a big cock and I am in no doubt it will work wonders between your buttocks. You seemed fairly keen for him to invite the young woman he mentioned. What little he told you of her sowed the seeds of an even greater orgy in your mind, am I right?

If you want, I will comply with this new whim and I shall ask him to arrange a meeting, but I shall not disguise the fact that it most likely will give me less pleasure because I am not keen to put some woman I do not know in your arms. Yes, darling Charles, you know that. I am jealous of you, terribly jealous, and it would be infinitely painful for me if I knew you were cheating on me. Alas, I know it does happen with your wife but I cannot help that and we can do nothing to change it. I have tolerated this situation for two years, but with another mistress . . . you know I could not cope with it. You see, you are so beautiful, my Charles, your glorious body is so thrilling, that I am afraid of another woman's desire for you, can you understand that? I want to keep you for myself, my darling treasure, and I am frightened . . . But at the end of the day, if it would really please you, I would do it anyway.

So I want you to tell me, my dear love, what pleasures I should bring to you. You know I would not back away from anything to satisfy your wildest perversity. I have seen just how much I love you, my darling lover, by sending you between the thighs of that beautiful bastard who made you come so intensely. Is his tongue more skilled than mine, then, my treasure?

Yesterday I brought myself to a climax twice as I thought back over the scene, and I also remembered the pleasure I derived from being in your arms, yours and his alike, as you took it in turns to suck my streaming cunt. My love, I wish you had fucked me passionately to make me come but you were too tired, I know that, and that is why I stopped myself coming. I did not want him to make me come, my adored one. I drew back and cuddled up to you so your soft skin could soothe my inflamed senses.

Yes, my adored lover, I want to have you all to myself in a few days' time. I want us to meet in our discreet little room. We can talk about that incredible day, and I will do everything in my power to make you as happy as he did.

If you really miss a man's touch, we shall try to find someone else. For you, I shall find a way to identify a suitable candidate and I shall bring him to you so you can suck his cock or have him bugger you right up to his balls.

You are a beautiful bastard, my love, do you know that? It was good, wasn't it, having that huge prick throbbing in your mouth? You had all of it between your lips, right up to the balls, and you sucked it so well. That nice hard tool disappeared down your throat and only the balls were left outside your mouth, which I kissed when it was still full of warm come. Isn't it wonderful sucking on a big cock? And you must now understand the pleasure I get sucking yours, my treasure. I shall stop now, it is late. You must have an aching erection, I imagine, reading this letter. Well then, tug yourself, my love. Masturbate yourself shamelessly, let the come jet out of your cock and trickle between your fingers. Then you can wipe them over your lips and imagine you have sucked off a beautiful bastard. I shall masturbate too and think of all these extravagances. Write me a long letter tomorrow, telling me how you feel and what you want. If I find it exciting you shall have an answer on Thursday, a really filthy answer, my love. Draw me a picture.

Goodbye, my darling treasure, I love you passionately. Goodbye, my lover whom I adore. I want your body, your lips, your hands on me. I wish you were beside me so we could commit a thousand excesses together. We shall soon, shan't we?

You really must love me, my Charles. You know that all my happiness comes from you and we have not yet exhausted all our love's resources. You will soon see, we still have such profound pleasures to enjoy, just by loving each other, with all our perversity.

Kissing your darling lips passionately.

Your Simone

Wednesday morning, five o'clock

Charles, is this the end, must I give you up for all eternity? Must I strike you out of my life having loved you so tenderly?

We confronted each other yesterday. We exchanged some very hard words, and I had to give way to avoid an outburst in public, but you can well imagine what I was thinking as I came home!

I wonder what all this means, and I am waiting for a clear and faithful explanation from you; the one you gave me does not appear to me to express the truth.

And what do you mean by forbidding me from telephoning you any more? I have never given my name at your office, and was even extremely surprised anyone knew it. But that need not change anything, for it strikes me they have grown quite accustomed to taking my messages these last two years. And the letters and *pneus* do not go unnoticed either.

No, there is some reason behind this. I know you have changeable moods, but, really, I should like to know where we stand, and whether we shall continue to be what we were up until barely a week ago.

270

My darling, if you have found another mistress who is more expert than I am, or some huge cock you can use at your will to bugger you, I still love you enough to make way to the lucky, happy bastard who will take my place to serve your greatest enjoyment and his own, but I do feel that having lavished you with my attentions for two years (or nearly), I have a right to some consideration from you, and that you should not take your leave of me in some Métro carriage.

You treated me most peculiarly this evening, admit it. And I was quite devastated when I alighted. I was perhaps not very pleasant, I confess, but that really is no reason to hurt me.

So then, to summarise, I shall wait for a reply to this letter, some word from you to set things straight.

I cannot believe that two years of memories like ours can vanish like that in a burst of anger. I would have preferred our quarrel to vanish in a burst of passion. So, Charles, our love is all down to you. I shall not try to stir any arousal in you which might influence your decision. You must look only to your heart for the answer, which I hope is the same as mine, for, despite my outward sulkiness, you could tell there was only one thing I wanted: to take you in my arms and press my lips to yours.

We are stupid to batter each other like this, and all for a letter that was never written. Oh, go on then, I shall write the wretched letter for you, if you like, for your every caress raises great tides of desire in me, and I should so like to describe them, but you will not hear them this evening, for you are unkind.

But understand this, Charles, I love you and I always suffer when I think everything could be over between us, and my name no longer sounds the same in your heart. And yet my lips have lost none of their skill, and oh, if you were beside me! But no, I cannot tell you such things this evening. I am too sad.

So I shall not telephone again, I shall wait. Do not take too long, I need to know, to know everything.

Simone

My dearly loved darling,
  This will be a sad missive, for my heart is filled with despair as I write. That certainly was not the sort of farewell I wanted between us on the eve of such a long separation, and the quick, cold kiss we exchanged in full view on the street was a far cry from the kisses which have so often been on our lips.

And when I saw how eager you were to leave me, I had to face the facts: we must stop deluding ourselves and each other. A crack has appeared in our love. Which of us made it? We shall never know but it does not matter.

I am not writing to you reproachfully, my darling, but asking for you to be honest. In the name of everything we have had between us, in the memory of all our wonderful times, I beg you to tell me where we now stand. As I sit here now, I do not actually know whether I shall see you again, for you have shown so little tenderness, so little enthusiasm the last few weeks that I am convinced it is all over between us. When we parted I was hoping for some word from you that might have given me new hope, but you said nothing, nothing but wishing me well for my journey. You did not even ask for my address.

So, you see, whatever I do, whatever I say to persuade you, nothing can reassure me, and I am leaving without having mended this little crack. But do you think that a love like ours is worth repairing? Is it already too late to heal the pain you have inflicted on me? The future depends on you alone, Charles. I ask this of your heart: think it over. See whether you have some affection or desire left for me. I do not believe you do, and that is why I am asking you to give me your answer.

If you have decided to put the last full stop at the end of our story and if you felt uncomfortable admitting it out loud, please have the generosity to say it in writing. If there is to be nothing left between us, I need to know straight away. It would be cruel to leave me still hoping if your mind is now emptied of thoughts of me. Far from you, I can try to heal and forget. It will be a painful wound but I would rather suffer than live in doubt. Spare me this torturous ordeal, Charles, and tell me the truth. Don't leave me here with this little thought hammering constantly inside my head. I would rather know and know immediately. If you seek out other loves, my dear little god, do still remember that I loved you passionately and I gave you two beautiful years of my life, the wildest and most heartfelt years. I subjected my body to torture for you, you cannot already have forgotten all the passions I satisfied. I meekly accepted your desires, whatever they might have been, and I never shied away from anything to give you greater pleasure. That deserves remembering every now and then.

Oh, I still love you so much, my dear treasure, and the terrible thought that I have lost you drives me mad. Never again touching your skin with my hands or my lips, dear Lottie, never again kissing your warm lips, never again stroking your magnificent body . . . Can you really turn your back so quickly on all our ecstasies, all my attentions? Remember how soft my lips felt on your skin, remember my mouth ardently pumping your hard, proud prick and harvesting the last drop of your come from the very depths of your balls. Oh yes, I loved sucking your cock, my treasure, and eating your arse, and I also liked offering up my rump for you to beat furiously or penetrate brazenly with your beautiful prick hardened by my skilful tongue as it trailed from the head down to the balls. I can just picture your ramrod. Right now I can see such clear images of you. I can see the head of your prick straining towards my lips, your fingers tensed around it, guiding it towards my mouth, and I think I can still hear you saying, 'Here, little bitch, suck me, suck my prick. Oh yes, it's good, darling, again, again.' Oh, he stiffened so much in my mouth, that great cock of yours, and oh, the streams of come you released down my throat! But I don't want to remind your unfaithful heart of all these things if you have decided to forget them. You know I shall never stop picturing our couplings and imagining new ones for us. The days are over when you used to delight in these suggestive writings. Perhaps you are reading others now?

You wanted to experience a man's brutal touch, to suck a cock, to be sucked by a man. I gave you that ultimate sensation. Is that what you now hold against me, and did I upset you in any way? If I did, my darling love, you know it was to please you. I was faithful to you throughout the two years of our affair, and I never stopped loving you for one moment.

Well, I shall stop now. I should like to ask you, as a final favour, not to leave me with this uncertainty. Write back whenever you like, whenever you can and whatever you want. I am waiting for your decision and I shall accept it without faltering if your heart has stopped beating in time with mine.

My dear little god, this letter was necessary. If I have spoken the truth, it will be the last letter you receive from me and we shall forget each other. If I am wrong, wrong again, you must tell me, and tell me what I should do.

Goodbye, my dear treasure. Forgive me, forget the diffi-cult times. Think only of my mouth on your cock, my lips on your arse, my cock between your buttocks, my filthy little Lottie.

Are you no longer my Lottie? Are you no longer my Charles? Am I no longer your beautiful bitch with her firm arse and her skilful mouth which was so good at making you come? Oh, there is so much I could say if you still wanted my love!

I shall stop by the post office on Monday or Tuesday. I hope you will have told me your decision.

I shall kiss your big dark eyes one last time, and your adorable mouth, because I love you with all my heart, and my heart is still full of you.

Your Simone

POSTSCRIPT

Like any reader finishing this book after sharing in Simone's torments and empathising with her despair, having discovered these letters I couldn't help but wonder about Charles's sudden disappearance which brought the correspondence to an abrupt end.

Like Simone, I then wondered whether he had gone off with the 'beautiful bastard' whom she had so generously – and fatefully – found for him, as if trying to hasten a break-up that she had long known was inevitable.

That's not my interpretation of the ellipsis we have instead of the words 'THE END' on the last page of this story. I have lived with Simone for nearly a year, as I tried to organise her letters, gathering together all the jumbled pages, and patiently attempting to put them in chronological order, and I feel I came close to her, almost a hundred years after her extraordinary, doomed love affair. I often pictured her reading back through a letter at random, pulling out a single page, then another, and shedding tears. In fact, particularly in the last letters, entire lines are partly erased, very probably by her tears.

The work didn't give me a retrospective gift of sight, but I do feel that the process of organising the letters brought me genuinely close to both protagonists. Of course, Charles appears only through Simone's writing, but we see enough of him to get to know him intimately (and, in my case, to form a fairly low opinion of him).

Eventually he had had enough of the relationship. Simone's love was a burden to him; her expectations, her resentments, her passionate declarations, her pain, the sacrifices she made, and even her libido, which delighted him at first, now all began to suffocate him. But he didn't have the courage to end the relationship, and he let himself be led on by his desire and the thrill of the new pleasures Simone offered, while hating her for his own weakness.

There is talk of a whole night in each other's arms: Charles promised this in 1929, and it is the only full night mentioned in the whole two-year affair, which was typified by furtive and mostly infrequent trysts. Some letters refer to this night as an imminent event, but not one describes it, and I doubt Charles ever actually granted Simone this pleasure. In the last few months he saw her only occasionally, he avoided her, and there were more and more arguments following their time together. So he continued the relationship with a weariness punctuated by occasional flashes of desire, because Simone was not merely in love: her passion made her skilful, and the more she felt he was slipping away, the more she fired him up with new fantasies, to the extent that she was the one who showed him he had a taste for men.

The only point, then, where fiction comes into this book is the end. Like me, the reader can interpret at will and give free rein to his or her imagination.

My view is that Charles couldn't bear the reflection of himself that he saw in this daring pursuit of his own ultimate cravings; and, now that he had decided to abandon Simone, he felt more comfortable convincing himself these extremes were not his fantasies but hers alone. He could therefore reject what in 1930 was an unenviable prospect: acknowledging his own homosexual tendencies which his besotted mistress had revealed to him in spite of himself.

Simone is the heroine of this love story, and Charles is merely a secondary character. Nearly a century later, even when Simone's passion has long since been buried with her, and Charles himself has been reduced to dust, Simone remains sublime and her suffering still haunts us. Perhaps that's why I was so peculiarly affected when I found the box in which the satchel was hidden under those empty jars and wads of old newspaper: the emotional charge was still there and still radiated an energy after decades of lying forgotten in a cellar. I would have liked to console her, to take her in my arms and tell her that her young lover wasn't worth so much torment, and that disappointment in love is always insignificant if we can only view it with the benefit of hindsight. I can just offer a pointless comforting hug to a fleeting ghost, but I do hope her story will touch readers, and that this will retrieve our heroine from obscurity and give her a whole new life.

In the end, it doesn't really matter why Charles disappeared abruptly from Simone's life. What remains and what matters is the wonderful illustration Simone gives us of the eternal nature of woman, and of an element of self-sacrifice which goes beyond the appetite for sexual possession and gratification described in these letters, and is integral to the way women have loved, do love now, and will continue to love.

JYB

... ,

Ceci sera un triste billet car à l'heure où je t'

e ... Ce n'est certes pas un adieu comme fut le

à la ville d'une aussi longue séparation et ce

te nous avons échangé en pleine rue, me ressent

te te souvient sur nos lèvres ....

Et je me suis rendue à l'évidence en voi

il ne faut plus nous leurrer l'un et l'autre.

quel est celui de nous deux qui l'a faite ?

mais qu'importe !

po
rie
que q
là ...
Je me
et je suis

sur moi, mon cher amour,

t noir au bout de ces quais

t de la main je t'adressais mes

e pouvais plus te voir ... pai

nous parcourions, l'en bas de

des repro
tout c
ure d
je t
su
is

de te rende
est celle qu
que tu et me
le désir de te
moy vice au
voudrais com
salaud.

nette chère, pourquoi e

tor, loin de tes lèvres.

ent triste et longtems

j'implacable que vou

ah! comme je t'aime

irrésistiblement

Ma proposé chère,

dis moi pourquoi je suis t
chagrin indéfini et j'ouvre n
les voiles .... Tout à l'heure
me tiendras tout près de ton
yeux et ta bouche tant aimée

Si tu savais comme il m
bras ... et tu savais combien
je te dois les plus belles heures de